BRITISH RAILWAYS

PAST and PRESENT

No 24

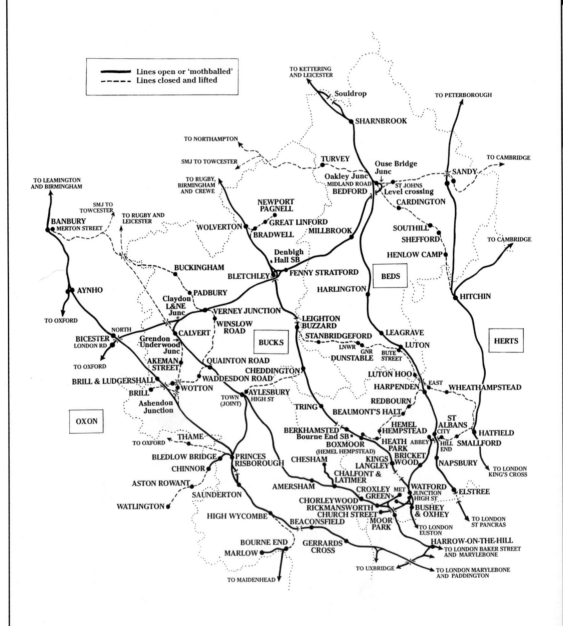

BRITISH RAILWAYS

PAST and PRESENT

No 24

Buckinghamshire, Bedfordshire and West Hertfordshire

Paul Shannon

Past and Present

Past & Present Publishing Ltd

First published in May 1995
Reprinted May 1996

British Library Cataloguing in Publication Data

A catalogue record for this book is available from the British Library

ISBN 1 85895 073 2

Past & Present Publishing Ltd
Unit 5
Home Farm Close
Church Street
Wadenhoe
Peterborough PE8 5TE
Tel/fax (0832) 720440

Maps drawn by Christina Siviter

Printed and bound in Great Britain

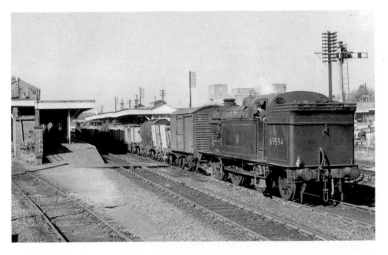

LUTON BUTE STREET: The Great Northern Railway reached Luton Bute Street from Welwyn in 1860, almost a decade before the Midland Railway opened its much more direct route between Luton and the capital. Both stations are visible in this photograph dated 30 September 1959. Class 'N2' 0-6-2T No 69594 departs from Bute Street with a mixed goods for Hatfield, while the austere architecture of the ex-Midland station, rebuilt between 1937 and 1940, stands on the horizon.

Today the ex-Midland station remains basically unchanged, but there is no trace of the former GNR line or station. *Stephen Summerson/ PDS*

CONTENTS

BIBLIOGRAPHY

A Regional History of the Railways of Great Britain
 (David & Charles):
 Vol 3 - Greater London *by H. P. White*
 Vol 9 - The East Midlands *by Robin Leleux*
 Vol 13 - Thames and Severn *by Rex Christiansen*
The Last Years of the Great Central Main Line
 by Robert Robotham (Ian Allan Ltd)
British Railways Pre-Grouping Atlas and Gazetteer
 (Ian Allan Ltd)

British Rail Track Diagrams *(Quail Map Company)*:
 No 3 - Western Region
 No 4 - London Midland Region

Past issues of Railway Magazine; Trains Illustrated/
 Modern Railways; Rail Enthusiast/Rail; The Railway
 Observer; Branch Line News.

ASTON ROWANT was one of two intermediate stations (there were also three halts) on the GWR Watlington branch. This delightful scene was captured on film on 12 June 1957 and shows ex-GWR 0-6-0 Pannier tank No 5766 making its scheduled call with the 1.54 pm departure from Princes Risborough.

The Watlington branch beyond Chinnor closed to passengers later in 1957 and to goods in 1961. The trackbed quickly returned to nature. *R. M. Casserley/PDS*

INTRODUCTION

The original intention was to produce a single 'Past and Present' volume covering the railways of Buckinghamshire, Bedfordshire, Hertfordshire and Essex, but as work progressed it became clear that there was far too much material to be compressed into a single volume. Therefore the present volume deals only with Buckinghamshire, Bedfordshire and western parts of Hertfordshire; a later volume will cover the railways of Essex and eastern Hertfordshire.

London was a magnet for railway routes in South East England right from the beginning of the railway age. As different railway companies competed for their share of key traffic flows between London and provincial centres, the Home Counties were soon crossed by a large number of radial routes based on London. Often these routes ran parallel to each other, but were situated only a few miles apart. By contrast, cross-country links between the radial routes were provided only in a piecemeal fashion, or in some cases not at all. Even a substantial town like Watford had no through railway routes other than the LNWR line to London. Luton fared almost as badly, in view of the fact that the Welwyn-Luton-Leighton Buzzard line was never worked as a through route.

Cutbacks and closures in the 1950s and 1960s re-emphasised the dominance of London on the Home Counties railway network. All the radial routes from London have remained open, and all have benefited from major investment at some time in the past 20 years. Daily commuting over longer and longer distances has become a way of life for thousands of people employed in central London, and stations that were built to serve quiet rural villages such as Harlington and Cheddington have acquired a new role as commuter railheads.

Most of the non-radial routes, on the other hand, suffered heavily from the Beeching axe, or in some cases were closed even before the much maligned Doctor appeared on the scene. By 1968, for example, there was no surviving railway route linking the ex-Great Northern and Midland main lines for a distance of over 80 miles, after the axe had fallen on the St Albans-Hatfield, Dunstable-Welwyn, Bedford-Hitchin and Bedford-Sandy lines. Other non-radial lines that no longer exist include Harpenden-Hemel Hempstead, Dunstable-Leighton Buzzard, Cheddington-Aylesbury, Watford-Rickmansworth and Bletchley-Bicester, while the cross-country line from Bletchley to Bedford has lost all but its local service. The only notable exception to this trend has been the ex-LNWR Watford-St Albans branch, which, having escaped closure threats on several occasions in the 1960s and 1970s, was finally electrified and given an enhanced service in 1988.

The traction and rolling-stock depicted in the 'past' photographs in this volume include examples from three of the four main pre-Nationalisation railway companies, plus the Metropolitan Railway, which later became part of London Transport. In some places there were complex agreements for joint working that led to an amazing variety of motive power in use at a single location. Perhaps the most striking example of this was at Aylesbury, where ex-LNER, ex-LMS and ex-GWR locomotives were all brought together in the British Railways era by the combination of express trains on the ex-Great Central main line and local services on the main line and on the branch from Princes Risborough.

In other parts of the Home Counties, working patterns established in the pre-Nationalisation era and in some cases even in the pre-Grouping era were remarkably resistant to change during the 1950s and 1960s. Cases of motive power transfers away from 'home' territory were generally rare. It was perhaps not until the running down of the 'Regions' and the setting up of BR business sectors in the 1980s that many anachronistic barriers between different companies' lines were finally broken down. Surely one of the most telling changes was the setting up of Thameslink, which, as well as making many new through journeys possible, allowed the London-Bedford service to be operated entirely by electric multiple units allocated to the former Southern Region. This would have been unthinkable 20 years ago.

Even now that the number of people commuting into Central London has apparently passed its peak, the basic passenger network within Buckinghamshire, Bedfordshire and Hertfordshire seems relatively secure. There have also been some interesting proposals to expand the network, although none has yet been given sufficient financial backing for a definite go-ahead. One is the possible re-opening and electrification of the line from Luton to Dunstable. It is tempting to speculate that this line might never have been closed if someone had thought to provide a suitable connection between ex-Midland and ex-GNR tracks at Luton back in the 1960s. Secondly there have been proposals for a new cross-country service between Swindon and Peterborough, which would use the currently mothballed Bicester-Bletchley line as well as providing an express service on the Bletchley-Bedford line. Thirdly, detailed preparatory work has paved the way for a possible new link between the virtually disused ex-LNWR Croxley Green branch and the ex-Metropolitan Watford branch with its poorly sited terminal station. This long-overdue link, while it will cost a lot of money, now seems the most likely of the three schemes to go ahead.

For revenue-earning freight traffic, the outlook is not particularly bright. In 1994 there were just six regularly operational freight terminals in the area covered by this volume, at Calvert (refuse disposal), Bletchley (roadstone), Stewartby (refuse disposal), Radlett (roadstone), Luton (motor vehicles) and Elstow (roadstone). Even just ten years ago there were more than twice as many as that. Long-distance freight still passes through the area on the ex-Midland and ex-LNWR main lines, but that too has diminished over the past decade. The general decline of freight by rail is shown graphically in this volume by several very recent 'past' photographs depicting what are now discontinued freight operations. Nevertheless there is one possible scheme for future expansion that is worthy of mention, even though it still has substantial hurdles to overcome. That is the proposal to reopen the Great Central main line as a through route for trainloads of HGV trailers between the Channel Tunnel and the East Midlands, making use of the comparatively generous loading gauge adopted by the Great Central Railway in the 1890s.

Compiling this volume brought many moments of sadness as I stood in the middle of a car park, or worse still amid a bed of nettles, trying to produce the modern counterpart to a 'past' photograph of a bustling railway scene. However. it was also fascinating to see some of the more subtle changes that have taken place on the surviving network, or to see in a few cases how remarkably little has changed over a period of perhaps 30 or 40 years. I am grateful to the many 'locals' who helped me to identify the right spot where there was doubt, just as I am to the many photographers who provided me with detailed caption information as well as with the 'past' photographs themselves. Special thanks must go to Stephen Summerson and Richard Casserley for their detailed checking of much of the manuscript. Any errors in this volume, however, are mine.

Paul Shannon
Chester and St Albans

The Midland main line

ELSTREE: The Midland main line between Bedford and London St Pancras was a relatively late addition to the British main-line railway network, not opening to traffic until 1867/68. Business was brisk, and the route was quadrupled in stages between 1875 and 1894. Freight was always in abundance, not least because the line offered the most direct route for coal trains from the East Midlands to London. On 27 June 1959 a delightfully mixed consist of mainly covered vans interspersed at random with the odd open wagon is whisked through Elstree & Borehamwood station by '9F' 2-10-0 No 92059.

All four tracks remain in use today, but with the emphasis on a greatly expanded suburban passenger service rather than heavy freight. Class '319' unit No 319047 is just arriving on the Down Slow line with the 14.57 Moorgate-St Albans service on 11 February 1994. The semaphore signalling was removed from Elstree in December 1979 under Stage 2 of the Midland main line resignalling scheme. *H. C. Casserley/PDS*

NAPSBURY station was a curious island platform located between the Up Slow and Down Slow running lines, built to serve the now closed adjacent mental hospital; it never had any goods facilities. A call has just been made there by Fowler 2-6-4T No 42334 on a down local service in 1949. The locomotive has just had its bodyside LMS initials painted out after passing into British Railways ownership; this was a cheaper alternative to a full repaint and was normal practice when locomotives received an intermediate repair. The track leading off to the right is the stub of a very short-lived connection between the Midland main line and the LNWR Watford-St Albans branch.

Napsbury was closed in September 1959, and today nothing remains of the station platform or buildings. Two Class '319' units speed past the site with a down Thameslink service on the evening of 2 August 1993. *Kevin Lane collection/PDS*

ST ALBANS CITY (1): A busy scene at the south end of St Albans station on 26 June 1958. On the right Standard Class '5' 4-6-0 No 73080 waits in the goods yard departure siding with the stock of a returning schools excursion to Fawkham on the Southern region. A 2-6-4T stands in the Up Slow platform with a local train to St Pancras, while a balancing northbound working pauses on the Down Fast.

On 2 August 1993 Class '319' No 319056 pulls away from a much modernised, rationalised St Albans station, forming the 13.48 Luton-Sutton service. After the closure of the goods yard in 1967, a parcels dock was retained on the up side of the station, but even that facility was withdrawn in 1979 and the area was subsequently fenced off for engineers' use. The down-side station buildings were demolished in the 1970s to make way for the inevitable car park, with replacement facilities provided on the up side of the station. *Michael Covey-Crump/PDS*

ST ALBANS CITY (2): A whole range of Steam Age paraphernalia on the station platform provides a nostalgic foil for '9F' 2-10-0 No 92028 as it passes St Albans on an up unfitted coal train on 23 March 1962. Of particular note is the brazier or 'fire devil' to the left of the water crane; this was filled with coke and lit during cold weather in an attempt to prevent the water in the crane from freezing.

Coal traffic through St Albans declined sharply in the 1970s and 1980s. In 1994 there are no regular coal trains on the southern half of the Midland main line at all, although a path still exists for occasional traffic to Ridham Dock. The main freight flows on the line today are connected instead with the construction industry, especially limestone from Leicestershire. Class '58' No 58049 heads south with the 08.37 Mountsorrel-Radlett limestone train on 16 February 1994. *Stephen Summerson/PDS*

LUTON (1): Standard Class '5' 4-6-0 No 73142 approaches Luton with a mid-morning down express on 11 March 1961. The locomotive carries the shed plate 17C, denoting its allocation to Rowsley. To the right of the signal box is the water softening plant, which supplied the water tank on the far right of the picture as well as the cranes in Crescent Road goods yard and at the platform ends.

Steam gave way to 'Peak' diesel-electrics, which had in turn given way to InterCity 125 sets on virtually all Midland main line InterCity services by the late 1980s. Power car No 43048 leads the 10.30 London St Pancras-Sheffield service into Luton on 6 August 1993. The mechanical signalling has long since been replaced by multiple-aspect colour lights controlled from West Hampstead in north-west London. The goods depot that once stood adjacent to the station has been demolished, although in fairness it should be added that Crescent Road yard to the south gained a new lease of life in 1994 as the loading point for Vauxhall cars to Bathgate. *Stephen Summerson/PDS*

LUTON (2): Originally Luton station had platforms only on the fast lines, plus an up-side bay for London-bound trains starting at Luton. The slow lines through the station were therefore effectively freight-only, and it was not until dieselisation in 1960 that through platforms were provided. Stanier 4-6-0 No 45238 of Cricklewood heads a fitted freight on the Down Slow line on 28 June 1961. By this time the former up bay, visible on the right-hand side of the photograph, had already had its track slewed over to join the Up Fast, and a connection had also been provided at the north end of the station in order to create a through loop.

Luton's track layout was altered yet again in 1978 in readiness for electrification. The Down Slow loop of 1961 became the main Down Slow line; the Down Through line became a reversible line used mainly by terminating EMUs; and the Up Slow line was slewed across to the east to allow construction of a new island platform. A Class '60'-hauled limestone train from Mountsorrel to Radlett takes the 'new' Up Slow line on 6 August 1993. *Stephen Summerson/PDS*

LUTON (3): This view shows the north end of Luton station before the track alterations of 1960, with the left-hand track still in use as an up bay. The new Up Slow platform can, however, be seen under construction on the right. Standard 9F 2-10-0 No 92109 of Leicester passes through with an up unfitted coal train on 21 April 1959. This Class was the mainstay of heavy freight workings at the time. With their larger tender tanks compared with older designs, they had the advantage of not needing to stop at Luton for water.

The 1960 Up Slow platform has come and gone, replaced in 1978 by the new island platform. Further changes came with resignalling and electrification, so that the scene is barely recognisable today apart from the curving tracks and the trees in the distance. Class '319' No 319170 enters the station with an up Thameslink service on 6 August 1993. *Stephen Summerson/PDS*

LEAGRAVE: Fairburn 2-6-4T No 42685 of Kentish Town calls at Leagrave with a midday local train to Bedford on 22 May 1957. At this time the four intermediate stations between Luton and Bedford - Leagrave, Harlington, Flitwick and Ampthill - had platforms only on the fast lines, and stopping trains north of Luton were irregular and infrequent. Long-distance commuting had yet to become established.

Leagrave, Harlington and Flitwick had their slow line platforms installed in readiness for dieselisation in 1960; Ampthill was less fortunate, closing completely in 1959. Dieselisation brought a regular hourly-interval service to the remaining three stations for the first time in their history. Today, with the benefits of electrification and Thameslink, Leagrave enjoys a more frequent service still: its basic off-peak frequency is four trains an hour, with some extras in the morning and evening peaks. Both fast and slow lines are used. On 6 August 1993 units 319174 and 319179 arrive with the 16.30 Brighton-Bedford service. *Stephen Summerson/PDS*

HARLINGTON: Still very much a country station serving a small village community, Harlington is pictured on 7 June 1939 with Johnson '3P' 4-4-0 No 757 passing through on the Down Fast with the 2.40 pm St Pancras-Kettering semi-fast, and Fowler '4F' 0-6-0 No 3967 (later BR No 43967) shunting the station goods yard. The Johnson 4-4-0s were withdrawn between 1925 and 1953, but many of the Fowler 0-6-0s survived into the 1960s.

Goods facilities were withdrawn from Harlington in 1967, but the solidly built Midland Railway goods shed has clearly been well looked after by its new owners. The original down-side station buildings remain in use, although partly masked by the clutter of electrification. The loss of goods traffic at Harlington has been more than compensated for by the phenomenal growth of commuting, plus the introduction of through services to places like Brighton and East Croydon that would have been unthinkable in LMS times. Class '319' unit No 319184 arrives with the 14.30 Brighton-Bedford service on 29 March 1994. *H. C. Casserley/PDS*

BEDFORD MPD: The original two-road locomotive shed at Bedford soon became inadequate and was replaced in 1886 by a longer, four-road shed on the western side of the new cut-off line avoiding Bedford station. The new shed is seen in the first picture on 19 March 1949 with three-cylinder Compound 4-4-0 No 41091 in attendance. The shed roof, with its 'northlight' pitch, was an unusual design for the Midland Railway, the only other large example being at Manningham. *H. C. Casserley*

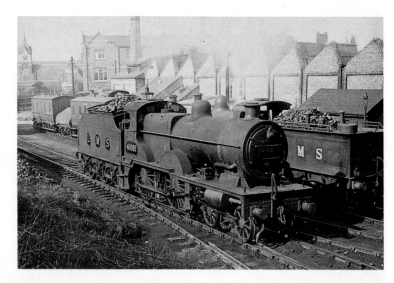

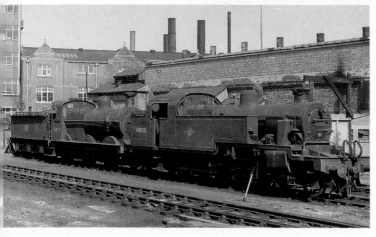

By 14 April 1962 the shed has been reroofed, as seen in the second view. The Compounds are no more, and even the two locomotives stabled there are in store pending disposal. On the right is Fowler 2-6-2T No 40020, formerly Bedford station pilot after a spell of push-pull work on the Watford-St Albans and Harrow-Stanmore branches. On the left is Johnson 0-6-0 No 43474, used latterly on the Bedford-Hitchin branch. No 43474 is a remarkable survivor of a class first introduced in 1890 and rebuilt from 1916 onwards. *Stephen Summerson*

Bedford shed lost its active allocation in July 1963, although it continued to be used by visiting locomotives for some time afterwards. Perhaps the most remarkable thing about the third picture, dated 1 January 1994, is that the shed is still standing, albeit derelict since the end of steam. *PDS*

BEDFORD MIDLAND ROAD station was located at an odd angle to the Midland main line and was served only by the slow lines, despite the fact that all other stations between Luton and Kettering had only fast line platforms. The reason is that the Midland main line when first opened in 1857 ran from Leicester via Bedford to Hitchin, where it joined the Great Northern main line for the final approach to London. When the Midland Railway opened its own independent route to London a decade later, the old Bedford station on the Hitchin line was retained and linked to the new line by a sharp curve to the south. New platforms were provided for the new line to London, but these were still on the Hitchin alignment. The original Hitchin tracks meanwhile were divided into two north-facing and two south-facing bays. About to depart from one of the former on 2 August 1958 is Ivatt 2-6-2T No 41272 with a push-pull train to Northampton. On the locomotive bodyside is a plate marking the fact that this was the 7,000th locomotive built at Crewe.

In December 1978 a new Bedford Midland Road station was opened closer to the 1894 cut-off alignment, although still without platforms on the fast lines. This allowed the old station site to be made available for car parking and redevelopment. The only link between the 1958 picture and the present-day scene is the pair of Victorian houses in Ashburnham Road. *Stephen Summerson/PDS*

OAKLEY JUNCTION, 2 miles north of Bedford, marked the divergence of the Midland Railway branch to Northampton. There was also a station named Oakley, located on the main line some distance north of the junction. Standard 4-6-0 No 75040 heads south on the main line with a morning Leicester-London St Pancras semi-fast working on 20 August 1960. This rather short formation would probably have had three suburban carriages added to it at Bedford.

All traces of the junction and crossovers have disappeared, as have the two sidings on the down side of the line. The multiple-aspect signalling is controlled from West Hampstead power box. An InterCity 125 set with power car No 43073 leading forms the 07.50 Sheffield-London St Pancras service on 1 January 1994. *A. N. Davenport/PDS*

SHARNBROOK: Three-cylinder Compound 4-4-0 No 41173 heads north through Sharnbrook station with the 2.50 pm London St Pancras-Nottingham relief train on 16 August 1958. By this time Compounds were rare performers on the main line, and the photographer recalls some anxiety in the Control Office as to whether No 41173 would keep time with its ten-coach load. Apparently it did.

Sharnbrook station was closed to passengers in May 1960 and to goods in May 1964. The signal box was closed in December 1987 at the same time as the track layout was remodelled, with all four lines retained south of Sharnbrook but only three to the north. Some Midland Railway fencing and the old goods shed provide a link to the present-day scene. *Stephen Summerson/PDS*

SOULDROP (SLOW LINES): When the Midland main line was extended south from Leicester in the 1850s, money was in short supply and wherever possible the engineers opted for cuttings and gradients rather than building tunnels. As a result, the original line climbs to an altitude of 315 feet at Sharnbrook summit (actually near the village of Souldrop), approached by 3 miles of 1 in 120 in the up direction and by a slightly less severe gradient in the down direction. Once the Midland had opened its direct line to London St Pancras, traffic volumes grew rapidly. From the late 1870s onwards, therefore, the company set about quadrupling its existing line between Kettering and Bedford. A gentler alignment was used for the additional tracks, with a maximum gradient of 1 in 200 for up trains and with a 1,860-yard tunnel at Souldrop beside the existing Sharnbrook summit. This made them much more suitable for the kind of heavy freight traffic that characterised the Midland main line. Standard '9F' 2-10-0 No 92021, with its original Crosti boiler, drifts down from the tunnel with an unfitted mixed goods train on 16 August 1958.

When the Midland main line was resignalled in the late 1980s, the extra tracks were reduced to a single reversible freight line between Sharnbrook and Harrowden, and removed altogether between Harrowden and Kettering. From a train pathing point of view it would have been possible to dispense even with the reversible line between Sharnbrook and Harrowden, but it was retained for use by those few freight trains that might still struggle to breast Sharnbrook summit. In the event, the summit has become less of a problem since the introduction of Class '60' locomotives, and the majority of freight trains on this stretch do in fact now use the fast lines. An exception to the norm, then, is this view of No 60015 *Bow Fell* heading south with the 09.57 Peak Forest-Bletchley stone train on 9 August 1993. *Stephen Summerson/ PDS*

SOULDROP (FAST LINES): Still something of a novelty on the Midland main line on 18 September 1961 is 'Peak' locomotive No D15, approaching Sharnbrook summit on the Down Fast with the 4.10 pm London St Pancras-Sheffield service. No D15 survived into the TOPS era as Class '45' No 45018, but was one of the first of its Class to be withdrawn in 1981.

'Peaks' gave way to InterCity 125 sets on the Midland main line without a great deal of ceremony in the early 1980s. Although the InterCity 125s were unable to use their full speed potential, they did produce some improved timings because of their faster acceleration, and they helped also to cultivate the InterCity image on a line often regarded as under-funded. The 13.00 London St Pancras-Nottingham service approaches the summit on 6 August 1993. *Michael Mensing/PDS*

Branch lines from Bedford

BEDFORD (HITCHIN LINE): Representing the last generation of rolling-stock to use the Bedford-Hitchin branch, a two-car Derby lightweight unit consisting of Driving Trailer No M56262 and Motor Brake 2nd No M50979 leaves Bedford with the 12.20 pm departure for Hitchin on 18 September 1961. This type of unit later became designated Class '108', and was one of the more successful first-generation DMU types, with many examples surviving into the 1990s. Of the two vehicles pictured here, No M50979 was an early victim of accident damage, but No M56262 spent its last days working from Longsight depot as No 54262 until final withdrawal in February 1992.

This northernmost section of the Hitchin branch, from Bedford to Cardington, was closed in 1969 and lifted shortly afterwards. Only the once rail-served brewery building serves as a present-day link with the old picture, and even that has been trimmed somewhat! *Michael Mensing/PDS*

SOUTHILL: The railway from Bedford to Hitchin was a main line for only the first ten years of its existence, ousted in 1868 by the Midland Railway's direct line to St Pancras. After 1868 it maintained a basic passenger service of four daily trains each way, increased to seven in 1958 when the first diesel railcars arrived. As so often, however, dieselisation did little to improve the line's performance, and it was closed to passengers in January 1962. Pictured on 5 March 1960 is the intermediate station at Southill, a particularly delightful example of Leicester & Hitchin Railway architecture.

Closure to passengers was followed by complete closure of the Cardington-Southill-Shefford section in December 1964. Happily, Southill station has been beautifully restored as a private house, with virtually every architectural detail retained in its original form. *Stephen Summerson/PDS*

HENLOW CAMP: After its demotion from main-line status, much of the Bedford-Hitchin line was reduced to single-track formation in 1911. Double track was retained only between Shefford and Henlow, effectively forming a long passing loop. Latterly Henlow Camp became one of the busier stations, serving an adjacent military base, and here the former down platform was lengthened to cater for special military trains. This scene is dated 28 May 1960, but probably not a lot had changed apart from platform lengthening in the previous 40 years!

The section from Shefford to Hitchin, including Henlow, was closed to all traffic in December 1963. Today the station area has been largely built over, and some help from an elderly local resident was necessary in order to find the correct spot. *Stephen Summerson/PDS*

The third picture shows an ex-LNER locomotive on this former LMS line. Although the regular branch service was always worked from the Bedford end, in later years there were also two leave trains each week, on Friday evenings and Saturday mornings, from Henlow Camp to London King's Cross, and these were worked by the Eastern Region. Class 'J15' 0-6-0 No 65479 - a design introduced in 1883! - is pictured arriving at Henlow with empty stock to work the Saturday morning departure to King's Cross on 28 May 1960. No 65479 was withdrawn in August 1960, at around the same time that the through trains from Henlow to King's Cross were discontinued. *Stephen Summerson*

TURVEY was one of three intermediate stations on the 21-mile Midland Railway branch from Bedford to Northampton. This line was opened to traffic in 1872 and ran initially to the Midland Railway's own terminus at Northampton St Johns Street; only in 1939 was a connection provided so that trains could run through to the principal LMS (ex-LNWR) station at Northampton Castle. Traffic was never particularly brisk, and the newly dieselised passenger service was withdrawn in March 1962. Stanier Class '5' 4-6-0 No 44691 passes light-engine through Turvey on the last day of passenger traffic, 3 March 1962.

Apart from a short section between Northampton and Piddington, retained until the 1980s to serve a military depot, the Bedford-Northampton branch was closed to all traffic in January 1964 and the track was lifted in the following year. Turvey station building is now in use as office accommodation for the Agricultural Division of Cargill plc. *Stephen Summerson/PDS*

SANDY: Destined to form part of the 77-mile cross-country link from Oxford to Cambridge, 3½ miles of railway from Sandy to Potton were opened in 1857, followed by the Bedford-Sandy and Potton-Cambridge sections five years later. The LNWR took over the route in 1865, linking up with its existing line from Bedford to Bletchley. At Sandy the LNWR line ran alongside the Great Northern main line for over a mile, but there was never a physical connection between the two lines, not even in BR days. A call at the ex-LNWR Sandy station is being made by a two-car Derby lightweight DMU on 7 August 1961, forming the 2.12 pm Cambridge-Bletchley service.

The ex-LNWR line between Bedford and Cambridge was closed to all traffic on 1 January 1968, except for a short section from Bedford to Goldington power station, which was retained for coal traffic into the early 1980s. The closure of the ex-LNWR Sandy station made it possible to eliminate, at long last, the troublesome double-track bottleneck at this point on the East Coast Main Line. Today's Up Slow platform, then, is located almost exactly on the trackbed of the former LNWR route. Class '317' unit No 317333 departs from the new platform with the 12.10 Peterborough-London King's Cross service on 25 March 1994. *Michael Mensing/PDS*

BEDFORD (OUSE BRIDGE JUNCTION): This stretch of line across the River Ouse originally formed part of the Bedford-Hitchin route. After the withdrawal of through services to Hitchin it remained busy with local shunting movements and also continued to provide access to the connecting line between the Midland main line and the Bedford-Bletchley line. The first view shows ex-'LMS' '3F' 0-6-0T No 47279 shunting an ex-Southern Railway parcels van at Ouse Bridge Junction on 14 April 1962. On the right is the characteristically busy ex-Midland Railway goods depot.

Almost two decades later, on 28 July 1981, some of the trackwork has been rationalised and Ouse Bridge signal box has been demolished. The goods depot warehouse still stands, although it is no longer used for its original purpose, and the sidings beside it have found a new use for stabling engineers' stock. Class '25' locomotives Nos 25266 and 25315 wait for a clear road into Bedford Midland Road station with the daily Fletliner service from Stewartby to Longsight and Garston. A similar trainload of containerised bricks ran also from Stewartby to London King's Cross, but both services were withdrawn shortly after the date of this photograph.

The third picture shows the scene at Ouse Bridge Junction on 6 August 1993. The trackwork has hardly changed at all since 1981, but the line regained its status as a passenger route in 1984 after the rerouting of Bedford-Bletchley line trains. Green-liveried single unit No 55023 is pictured forming the 16.20 departure from Bedford to Bletchley. *Stephen Summerson/PDS (2)*

BEDFORD ST JOHNS (1): The first railway to reach Bedford was the branch from Bletchley, opened in 1846 by th
London & Birmingham Railway company to a terminus at Bedford St Johns. That terminus became a through sta
tion in 1862 when the line was extended from Bedford to Cambridge. The first photograph shows St Johns in mor
or less its original condition on 7 May 1956, with Class '4F' 0-6-0 No 43841 standing in the eastbound platform wit
a train from Bletchley. The first carriage in the train is fitted with vacuum-operated retractable steps, necessary a
this time because some of the intermediate stations between Bedford and Bletchley had no raised platform.

The present-day scene is one of dereliction, with just the roofline of some houses on the right confirming th
correct location. *A. N. Davenport/PDS*

BEDFORD ST JOHNS (2): When through services were withdrawn between Oxford and Cambridge in 1968, the middle section between Bletchley and Bedford managed to retain its local passenger trains, mainly because some of the small communities along the line would be difficult to serve by road. In the 1970s and 1980s, however, the line was never far away from the threat of closure, with its revenue consistently falling short of day-to-day operating costs by a horrendous margin. Some economies had been achieved by withdrawing staff from Bedford St Johns station, pictured here on 28 July 1981 with a Cravens two-car DMU arriving from Bletchley. But St Johns was poorly sited, and the decision was taken shortly after the date of this photograph to divert trains over the existing freight-only link into Bedford Midland Road station instead. The last train from the old St Johns duly departed on 12 May 1984, and the new service to Midland Road via a new St Johns Halt (see overleaf) began two days later.

Nearly a decade after closure, the lamp for the former foot crossing is a curious survivor, while birch and willow trees have quickly colonised both trackbed and platform. Even more curious is the survival of Bedford St Johns signal box. Although the tracks beside it have long since been torn up, it still controls movements on the curve behind it known as the 'Bletchley angle', and acts as a fringe box to West Hampstead power box. *Both PDS*

BEDFORD ST JOHNS (NEW STATION): Ex-LMS '3F' 0-6-0T No 47279 shunts one ex-Southern Railway parcels va**r**
two BR standard mineral wagons loaded with domestic coal and one empty BR standard open wagon on the spu**r**
between the Midland and LNWR stations on 18 September 1961.

This previously freight-only link gained a regular passenger service in May 1984 when the old Bedford St John**s**
station was closed and trains from Bletchley were extended over the spur to terminate at the Midland main lin**e** station, calling also at a ne**w** Bedford St Johns Halt. Networ**k** SouthEast-liveried single unit N**o** 55027 approaches the new ha**lt** while working the 17.40 Bedfor**d–** Bletchley service on 6 August 199**3.** These single units are, at the tim**e** of writing, the standard rollin**g** stock in use on the line, with a tot**al** of four vehicles allocated t**o** Bletchley depot. *Michael Mensing*/ *PDS*

MILLBROOK is one of the succession of small stations and halts between Bedford and Bletchley, and provides a good example of the 'half-timbered Gothic' style of architecture that still characterises the line today. Apparently the style was used at the insistence of the Duke of Bedford whose estates the line traversed. Several of the stations had LNWR open frames instead of conventional signal boxes, as pictured here on the right. The open frame would have already been regarded as an interesting relic from the past when the photograph was taken on 13 April 1959.

There have been remarkably few major changes in the 35 years that separate the two photographs. The signalling and crossing gates have been replaced on a like-for-like basis, and the station building is still occupied even though it is no longer possible to buy a ticket there. *H. C. Casserley/PDS*

FENNY STRATFORD is the last station before Bletchley on the line from Bedford. The first photograph shows the station in April 1950, with a new eastbound platform under construction.

The line through Fenny Stratford was later singled in connection with track alterations for the Bletchley flyover and the 'new' platform had therefore only a relatively short life. However, the station building, signal box and semaphore signalling all survive to the present day, as shown by this view of single unit No 55027 arriving on the 14.40 Bedford-Bletchley service on 9 August 1993. Although the Bedford-Bletchley line has often been regarded as a thorn in the side by its operator Network SouthEast - it scarcely qualifies as a busy London commuter route, after all! - it has survived many threats of closure and has enjoyed since 1988 an enhanced service of one train an hour throughout the day. *Tom Middlemass/PDS*

West Coast Main Line, Bushey to Tring

BUSHEY TROUGHS: The southern-most section of today's West Coast Main Line, from London Euston to Boxmoor, was opened in 1837 by the London & Birmingham Railway (L&BR). Through running to Birmingham became possible in the following year; initially there were six daily trains each way between London and Birmingham, with the fastest taking 5 hr 37 min. The line was progressively quadru-pled as far as Bletchley between 1859 and 1876, and two further tracks were added between Euston and Watford between 1913 and 1922 to complete today's six-track formation. The photograph shows the original 'Princess Coronation' Class 'Pacific', No 46220 *Coronation*, taking water at Bushey troughs with the down 'Royal Scot' in 1960.

Today the first 16 miles of railway out of Euston remain one of the longest sections of six-track formation in the country, and all tracks are well used. The latest generation of motive power is represented by Class '90' No 90012 *British Transport Police* heading north with the 10.35 London Euston-Carlisle service on 27 October 1993. *H. G. Forsythe/PDS*

BUSHEY: The station at Bushey & Oxhey once had six platforms, four on the main alignment and two on the curve to Watford High Street for the local DC electrified lines. Fairburn 2-6-4T No 42159 pulls away from Bushey after making a call at the Down Slow platform with the 5.21 pm Broad Street-Tring service on 23 June 1952.

By the date of the present-day picture, 27 March 1994, the fast line platforms in the foreground have fallen into disuse, and even the slow line platforms are used only in the rush-hour by three trains each way; passengers at other times of the day must use the DC lines. Passing through at speed on the Down Slow is an eight-car Class '321' formation, headed by unit No 321434, working the 14.54 London Euston-Northampton service. *H. C. Casserley/PDS*

WATFORD JUNCTION (1): Stanier 'Black 5' 4-6-0 No 44751, fitted with Caprotti valve gear, pilots 'Jubilee' 4-6-0 No 45674 *Duncan* through Watford Junction on a wet 9 August 1952, hauling a London Euston-Manchester London Road express. In the foreground are the so-called local lines, which reached Watford Junction in 1913. They were electrified at 630 volts DC in 1917, initially for use by Bakerloo line underground trains, then, from 1922 onwards, by the full LNWR service from Euston and Broad Street.

Class '86' No 86245 approaches Watford Junction on a similarly dismal 27 October 1993 with the 09.40 London Euston-Wolverhampton service. The masts, gantries and wires associated with AC overhead electrification completely changed the face of Watford Junction in the mid-1960s, while the manual signalling of the earlier photograph - semaphores on the main lines and searchlight signals on the local lines - has given way to the multiple-aspect variety. The local line platforms have been rationalised so that only three of the original five are in regular use today. Interestingly, the DC tracks retain a fourth rail, although this is no longer necessary since the withdrawal of Bakerloo line trains north of Harrow & Wealdstone in the 1980s. *Brian Morrison/PDS*

WATFORD JUNCTION (2): Stanier 4-6-0 No 45003 approaches Watford Junction on the Up Slow line with the 8.00 am Northampton-London Euston local on 13 August 1949, framed by a splendid example of LNWR lower quadrant signalling; the footbridge at the north end of the platforms dictated the need for co-acting arms.

Today the local service between Northampton and London is much more frequent than it ever was in steam days, with three trains an hour for most of the day. Class '321' units Nos 321404 and 321401 arrive with the 14.00 departure from Northampton on 27 March 1994. The signalling on the 26-mile stretch between Kenton and Cheddington is now controlled remotely from Watford Junction panel. *H. C. Casserley/PDS*

WATFORD JUNCTION MPD: Situated next to the north end of Watford Junction's Up Slow platform, this six-road locomotive shed was responsible in its latter years for local duties on the St Albans branch and some trains to Euston, plus local engineering duties. The shed was built in two stages: first the hipped-roof section on the left, then the ridge-and-furrow section on the right. Ivatt 2-6-0 No 46470 is pictured outside the shed on 27 September 1962. This particular Class once totalled 128 locomotives. Although they were an LMS design and numbered in the ex-LMS series, many were built after Nationalisation and allocated to depots on non-LMS territory such as Darlington and Edinburgh St Margarets. No 46470 spent only a short period of its career at Watford; it was delivered in 1951 to West Auckland and withdrawn in 1967 from Carlisle Kingmoor.

Today the nearest locomotive servicing facilities to Watford are located at Willesden and Bletchley. Meanwhile the site of Watford shed has been subsumed into the huge station car park that now also encroaches on the original route of the St Albans branch (see page 54). *Stephen Summerson/PDS*

KINGS LANGLEY, where two generations of freight haulage are depicted. Stanier '8F' 2-8-0 No 48247 approaches Kings Langley on the Up Slow with a partially fitted mixed freight train in the early 1960s - masts are already in place for the impending electrification. The Stanier '8Fs' were among the very last steam locomotive types to survive in BR stock, with no fewer than 165 examples still active at the end of 1967.

Since the 1960s the southern stretch of the West Coast Main Line has seen a sharp reduction in freight traffic, particularly the bulk flows of coal and minerals, which have either been diverted or lost altogether. In 1994 a day

spent at Kings Langley (what a thought!) would most likely produce just a handful of Freightliner and train-ferry services. This rather poorly loaded train is 4L76, the 08.56 Crewe-Felixstowe Freightliner service, hauled by Class '86' locomotives Nos 86623 and 86621 on 27 October 1993. Although the Class '86s' have been a common sight on the West Coast route since 1965, it was only in 1978 that they were first allowed to work in tandem south of Rugby, allowing increased loadings for Freightliner trains.
Michael Covey-Crump/PDS

BOXMOOR (HEMEL HEMPSTEAD): Ex-LNWR rebuilt 'Precursor' '3P' 4-4-0 No 25319 *Bucephalus* approaches Boxmoor station with the 4.02 pm London Euston-Northampton train on 10 July 1939. The LNWR 4-4-0s were reduced to just eight examples by 1942, and No 25319 itself was withdrawn from service in December 1940. On the left is a characteristically busy station goods yard of the period, while on the right are examples of the massive suburban expansion of the 1930s that was to transform many small country villages that happened to lie on the path of the railway into major dormitory towns.

   Boxmoor was later renamed Hemel Hempstead in honour of the large community that it actually served, rather than the small one in which it was located. The goods facilities were withdrawn in 1966 as part of the general run-down of wagonload freight. However, the yard remained in use for parcels traffic, and it even gained a new plat-form and handling shed in 1979/80 when business was transferred here from Luton. Not until the early 1990s did the sight of an electric locomotive shunting two or three vans in the yard finally pass into history. With much of the now disused track-work still in place, Class '321' unit No 321427 enters Hemel Hempstead with the 14.54 London Euston-Northampton service on 13 February 1994. *H. C. Casserley/PDS*

BOURNE END is located roughly half-way between Hemel Hempstead and Berkhamsted stations. There was never a station here, just a set of crossovers between the slow and fast lines controlled by a signal box on the down side obscured by the steam. On 11 July 1939 a down express is whisked past by the combination of three-cylinder Compound 4-4-0 No 1092 and 'Royal Scot' 4-6-0 No 6138. These locomotives later became BR Nos 41092 and 46138 respectively.

By 13 February 1994 all traces of pointwork have long since disappeared from Bourne End. Driving Van Trailer No 82125 leads a rake of Mk2f carriages with a Class '87' locomotive bringing up the rear, forming the 14.50 London Euston-Preston service. Normally the DVT would be at the south end of the train; the arrangement pictured here is probably the result of an earlier unplanned diversion involving a reversal. *H. C. Casserley/PDS*

BERKHAMSTED (1): The LNWR signal box and lower quadrant semaphore greet 'Royal Scot' 4-6-0 No 6161 as it passes Berkhamsted with an up express on 19 August 1939. The 'Royal Scots' were characteristic West Coast Main Line express passenger engines from the late 1920s until withdrawals started in earnest in the early 1960s. It was fellow 'Royal Scot' No 6113 that made a world record run by taking a taking a train non-stop from London to Glasgow in April 1928, a distance of 401½ miles.

The 07.30 Manchester Piccadilly-London Euston service passes the same spot on a very dreary 31 December 1993. *H. C. Casserley/PDS*

BERKHAMSTED (2): Ex-LNWR 'Prince of Wales' 4-6-0 No 25827 enters Berkhamsted station on 11 July 1939 with the 10.14 Northampton-London Euston stopping train. Five members of the 'Prince of Wales' Class survived into British Railways days, although none was ever renumbered. No 25827 was one of the last two examples to be withdrawn from Bletchley shed in March 1948. The Class was replaced by 'Black 5s' on the main line and by 2-6-4Ts on the branches.

The 'Black 5s' gave way to AM10 (later Class '310') electric multiple units in April 1966, followed by a brief spell with Class '317' units in 1987/88 until the introduction of today's Class '321' units in 1989. An eight-car formation comprising units Nos 321402 and 321425 arrives at Berkhamsted on 31 December 1993 with the 09.31 Milton Keynes Central-London Euston service. The goods yard was closed in February 1967 and soon found a more profitable role as the station car park. It is rarely as empty as in this New Year's Eve photo! *H. C. Casserley/PDS*

TRING was for many years a terminating station for local trains from London Euston, despite its remoteness from Tring village centre. This view, dated 3 August 1944, shows the up-side carriage sidings well filled with suburban stock.

After electrification in 1966 most suburban trains were extended to Bletchley, and Tring became simply an intermediate calling point. Today it is served mainly by the half-hourly stopping service between London and Milton Keynes, although there are still a few rush-hour workings that terminate here. The 09.50 London Euston-Preston InterCity service passes through on the Down Fast line on 31 December 1993. *H. C. Casserley/PDS*

WATFORD JUNCTION (ST ALBANS BRANCH PLATFORM): Until the end of the 1960s, St Albans branch trains used the old No 10 bay platform at Watford Junction. Stanier 0-4-4T No 41901 is pictured there on 9 April 1958, shortly before departure with the 4.15 pm service to St Albans. On the left is the old No 11 platform, which was used by any main-line trains requiring access to the branch, such as excursions. On the right are the main-line through platforms complete with a Bakerloo line train in the down-side bay, which at this time extended the full length of the station.

The old No 10 platform was closed in 1970 and the tracks were removed to make way for a much-needed station car park. St Albans branch trains were then transferred to the adjacent No 11 platform (subsequently renumbered No 10!). However, even the new car parking facilities were soon found to be inadequate, and in 1973 a further extension led to the rerouting of the St Albans branch track some distance to the east, terminating at a new platform linked by a walkway to the main station. After this date the 'new' No 10 platform became a terminal platform for rush-hour trains to and from London Euston, as seen in the 'present' picture dated 27 October 1993. *David Holmes/PDS*

BRICKET WOOD: The first railway to reach the city of St Albans was the LNWR branch from Watford Junction, opened in 1858; it would be another decade before the Midland Railway provided Albanians with a more direct link to London. The 6½-mile branch was built as a single track, with one intermediate passing loop at Bricket Wood added by the LNWR in 1913. This view shows a pair of branch push-pull trains pausing for custom at Bricket Wood on 23 July 1955, with Fowler 2-6-2T locomotives Nos 40010 (left) and 40043 (right) in charge. This was offi-

cially the last day of steam operation on the branch, although, as the Watford Junction photograph shows, that isn't quite how things turned out in practice!

As a means to cutting costs and averting possible closure of the branch, the Bricket Wood passing loop was removed in the mid-1960s. All signalling was removed, and the branch became effectively one long siding from Watford Junction. More recently, however, the fortunes of the branch have risen with 25kV electrification, new rolling-stock and even a new intermediate halt at How Wood. Class '321' unit No 321422 represents the new order at Bricket Wood on 18 February 1993, forming the 11.50 service from Watford Junction. *Michael Covey-Crump/PDS*

ST ALBANS ABBEY (1): The LNWR station, which became known as St Albans Abbey, is pictured on 23 July 1958, with Fowler 2-6-2T No 40010 ready to depart with the 3.16 pm service to Watford Junction. The station buildings and overall roof did not have long to go, as the branch was reduced to 'paytrain' operation and all resident staff were withdrawn in January 1966. On the right is St Albans gasworks, for which sidings were retained until 1972.

A single platform and rudimentary waiting shelter is all that awaits passengers arriving on the 10.50 service from Watford Junction on 28 March 1993, formed by Class '321' unit No 321419. The land once occupied by the run-round loop and sidings has been sold off for speculative commercial development. At one stage the station site itself was to be redeveloped and the platform moved a few hundred metres down the line; thankfully that proposal, which would have meant a longer walk for most passengers, has been averted. *Michael Covey-Crump/PDS*

ST ALBANS ABBEY (2): The St Albans Abbey branch was used to try out some of the very first diesel multiple units introduced by BR. The first trials in 1952 involved a trio of ACV four-wheeled demonstration vehicles. Three years later the branch hosted another batch of four-wheeled railbuses built by the British United Traction Company (BUT). A formation of BUT vehicles waits at the St Albans terminus on 19 April 1958.

The BUT railbuses have long since been withdrawn, although diesel working on the branch was to persist for another 30 years, until the 25kV overhead electrification scheme was commissioned in July 1988. *Michael Covey-Crump/PDS*

SMALLFORD: The Great Northern Railway provided St Albans with its second railway. Its branch from Hatfield was opened as far as St Albans London Road in 1865, with trains running through to the St Albans LNWR terminus from 1866 onwards. One of the line's four intermediate stations, Smallford, is pictured on 12 March 1961, with Midland Railway-design '4F' 0-6-0 No 44575 heading an eastbound Branch Line Society special.

The Hatfield to St Albans line became an early casualty of road competition and its passenger services were withdrawn as long ago as 1951. Freight services, however, lingered on until the mid-1960s. The track was lifted between St Albans Abbey and Colney Heath Lane in 1966/67 and from the rest of the branch in 1968. *Michael Covey-Crump/PDS*

HILL END: Eight years after closure to passengers, the remnants of Hill End station greet LNER 'N7' 0-6-2T No 69632 as it heads light towards the Salvation Army print works siding near St Albans on 29 September 1959. It will return with the Tuesdays-only consignment of *War Cry* magazines for feeding into the national wagonload network at Hatfield; the traffic would normally amount to two or three van-loads. *Michael Covey-Crump*

Today most of the formation between St Albans and Hatfield has been made into a public footpath and cycle track. *PDS*

The third picture, taken from a slightly different viewpoint, shows a display board with information about the line, plus some buildings on the former trackbed that provide temporary accommodation for homeless people. *PDS*

BEAUMONT'S HALT: The 8-mile branch line from Harpenden to Hemel Hempstead was opened in 1877 and operated by the Midland Railway. Originally trains ran between Luton and Hemel Hempstead via a north-facing curve
at Harpenden, but the service was diverted via a new south-facing curve into Harpenden station in 1888.
Beaumont's Halt was one of three additional halts provided when the Midland Railway introduced a rail-motor
service between Harpenden and Hemel Hempstead in 1905. The others were Godwin's, between Beaumont's and
Hemel Hempstead, and Heath Park, three-quarters of a mile beyond Hemel Hempstead. It looks in surprisingly
good order in this view taken on 21 April 1956, some nine years after the end of regular passenger services.

Today much of the former Hemel Hempstead branch has been made into a public footpath, formally opened on
1 December 1985. However, a short section west of Redbourn now forms part of the B487 by-pass road, pictured
here on 13 February 1994. *Stephen Summerson/PDS*

REDBOURN was the only settlement of any importance along the route, but passenger carryings dwindled, and regular passenger trains ceased in 1947. A South Bedfordshire Locomotive Club special is seen crossing the A5 at Redbourn on 24 September 1960, hauled by Fowler 2-6-2T No 40026. This locomotive was allocated to St Albans shed and normally worked suburban trains to and from Moorgate.

General freight traffic on the so-called 'Nicky line' through Redbourn persisted until 1963, after which the only user of the line was the Hemelite factory at Cupid Green on the outskirts of Hemel Hempstead. Hemelite purchased the line from BR in 1968, then used its own locomotives, including an ex-BR 'Clayton' from 1973 onwards, to transport wagonloads of ash between the main-line junction at Harpenden and its Cupid Green factory. However, the traffic was small in volume and involved using an awkward facing turnout on the Down Fast at Harpenden, which BR wanted to abolish under the Midland main line resignalling scheme. The branch therefore closed completely with effect from 1 July 1979. *Michael Covey-Crump/PDS*

HEMEL HEMPSTEAD MIDLAND ROAD: Ivatt 2-6-0 No 43118 arrives at Midland Road station on the afternoon of Saturday 30 May 1962 with the daily pick-up goods train from Harpenden; the traffic was stationery products from the local Dickinson's factory. No 43118 is about to take water from a hose on the platform and will then exchange its empty vans for loaded ones in the yard behind the station building.

To accept that this is the same location today takes some believing. But it is. After closure of the railway, the road was straightened out and now crosses the former trackbed slightly to the west of the original bridge alignment. *Stephen Summerson/PDS*

ST ALBANS CITY: Recalling the long-forgotten days of 'Rail blue' and the inviolable BR corporate image, Class '45' 'Peak' No 45070 passes St Albans City with a 'merry-go-round' coal train for Northfleet cement works on 21 September 1979. The up side parcels dock is still in daily use.

Within a year of the 'past' photograph the scene had been changed by the erection of overhead catenary and the replacement of semaphores by colour lights. The parcels facilities were also soon to be withdrawn. No 45070 lasted until the mid-1980s in revenue-earning service, while the last feature of the old photograph to disappear was the coal traffic to Northfleet, coming to an end in 1992. The present-day scene shows Class '319' unit No 319030 departing as the 10.03 Bedford—Sevenoaks service on 29 March 1994. *Both Paul Shannon*

NAPSBURY is pictured on 17 September 1979, with preparatory work for resignalling and electrification in progress. Crossing over from the Up Slow to the Up Fast line is an engineers' train with Class '25' No 25277 at the front and sister locomotive No 25176 at the rear. The photograph emphasises the kink in the Up Slow line and the unusual positioning of Napsbury signal box, both brought about because there was once an island platform here between the two Slow lines.

No-one would ever guess today that there had once been an island platform station at Napsbury. A mid-morning InterCity 125 service for London St Pancras speeds past on 29 March 1994. *Both Paul Shannon*

LUTON BUTE STREET station is pictured on the last day of operation, 24 April 1965, with a two-car Cravens diesel multiple unit about to depart for Welwyn Garden City. The first DMUs had been introduced to the line in September 1962, just after the ex-LNWR section of the route from Dunstable to Leighton Buzzard had been closed.

In 1994 the motor car reigns supreme! The track through the former Bute Street station was removed in 1992, instantly stifling plans to bring the Dunstable branch back into use for steam locomotive crew training, and making it seem less likely that the branch will ever be reopened to passengers. *Stephen Summerson/Paul Shannon*

GREAT LINFORD: Long before this part of rural Buckinghamshire became enveloped by Milton Keynes new town, Ivatt 2-6-2T No 41222 sets off from Great Linford with the 1.30pm Newport Pagnell-Wolverton train on 26 October 1963.

In July 1994 the scene at Great Linford is still green, although the course of the railway is now flanked by a mixture of parkland and housing instead of farmland. The former trackbed has been made into a pleasant walkway and cycle track. *Michael Mensing/Paul Shannon*

LEIGHTON BUZZARD: Stanier '8F' No 48550 comes off the Dunstable branch with a short mixed goods train on 1 May 1963.

Thirty-one years later all traces of the goods yard and branch line to Dunstable have long since vanished. The growth in long-distance commuting from the 1960s onwards is shown graphically by the number of cars in the car park, as well as by the lengthened station platforms. *Stephen Summerson/Paul Shannon*

WATFORD JUNCTION: Stanier rebuilt 'Royal Scot' 4-6-0 No 46146 *The Rifle Brigade* storms through Watford Junction with a lengthy up parcels train on 27 October 1962. No 46146 was withdrawn from stock only a few weeks afterwards, its West Coast Main Line duties taken over by diesels until the completion of electrification in 1966.

Watford Junction station was rebuilt and the footbridge removed in the mid-1960s. The result is a rather nondescript but functional modern station, now overshadowed by a 1980s office development visible on the far left of the photograph. A '92xxx' Driving Van Trailer heads the 15.30 Manchester Piccadilly-London Euston service into the station on 17 June 1994, with a Class '90' locomotive bringing up the rear. *Stephen Summerson/Paul Shannon*

BICESTER NORTH: 'Hall' Class 4-6-0 No 4907 *Broughton Hall* arrives at Bicester North station on 31 May 1960 with the 4.34 pm semi-fast train from London Paddington to Wolverhampton High Level. This train waited at Bicester until the passage of the 5.10 Paddington-Wolverhampton express, which had a slip coach dropped from it for attachment to the 4.34 service.

The same view is illustrated on 24 March 1994, with Class '165' unit No 165026 pulling away from Bicester North as the 17.30 Banbury-London Marylebone service. Goods facilities were withdrawn from Bicester North in 1964, and in 1968 the line was singled except for a passing loop in the station. After 1968 the 'North' suffix was no longer necessary, as Bicester's other station, on the ex-LNWR route to Oxford, had closed down, but the suffix was reapplied in 1987 when passenger services to Oxford resumed. *Michael Mensing/Paul Shannon*

CHESHAM: Although the Chesham branch was never owned by British Railways, trains on it were hauled by British Railways locomotives until the commissioning of electrification in 1960. The live rails provide a contrast with the water crane in this view of the Chesham terminus dated 21 August 1960. Ivatt 2-6-2T No 41284 is just arriving with the branch train from Chalfont & Latimer.

Much rationalisation and modernisation has taken place at Chesham by the date of the second photograph, 13 February 1994. A train of A60 stock arrives with the 14.00 departure from Chalfont. *R. C. Riley/Paul Shannon*

HEATH PARK: The last 2 miles of the former Midland Railway branch, between Hemel Hempstead and Boxmoor, had a curious history. Looking at the map today it would be tempting to assume that through services operated to and from the LNWR at Boxmoor, but this in fact never happened. Heath Park Halt, pictured here on 5 May 1956, was the westerly limit of passenger services from Harpenden. Freight operations were similarly organised from the Harpenden end. These included coal to Cotterills depot, reached by means of the siding on the left, and coal to Boxmoor gasworks, just west of Heath Park and tantalisingly close to the ex-LNWR main line. In 1959 the railway between Hemel Hempstead Midland Road and Boxmoor gasworks was closed, and a connection was at last provided into the gasworks from the LNWR end. But this lasted only a matter of months as the gasworks closed in 1960!

Virtually all traces of the Midland Railway route through Hemel Hempstead were swept away in the 1960s to allow redevelopment and the construction of one of the country's first two-way roundabouts. Only the houses in the distance provide a positive link between the two pictures, while the road in the foreground is a widened version of the one hidden underneath the bridge parapet in the old picture. *Stephen Summerson/PDS*

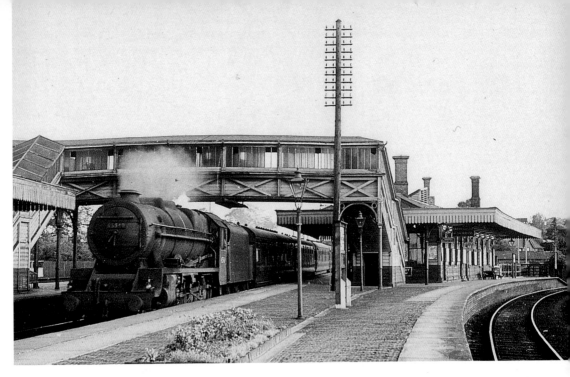

West Coast Main Line, Cheddington to Wolverton

CHEDDINGTON: Ex-LMS 'Patriot' 4-6-0 No 45540 *Sir Robert Turnbull* passes Cheddington on the Down Fast line with the 6.00 pm London Euston-Manchester London Road express on 4 August 1949. No 45540 was one of 18 'Patriots' to be rebuilt from 1946 onwards with a larger taper boiler, new cylinders and a double chimney. Curving round to the right is the branch to Aylesbury.

Forty-four years later Cheddington retains what appears to be its original iron footbridge, but the attractive LNWR station buildings have been replaced by a rather ugly modern structure. The Aylesbury branch is but a distant memory as a pair of Class '321' units approaches the Down Slow platform with the 10.04 London Euston-Milton Keynes Central service on 31 December 1993. *H. C. Casserley/PDS*

CHEDDINGTON (AYLESBURY BRANCH): The 7-mile line from Cheddington to Aylesbury is usually regarded as the earliest branch line in British railway history. It was opened by the London & Birmingham Railway in 1839, amid much celebration and with the opening day declared to be a public holiday in the Buckinghamshire county town. For the next quarter of a century the branch thrived as it provided Aylesbury with its only railway access, but its fortunes were dented first by the opening of the GWR branch from High Wycombe in 1863, then even more severely by the opening of the direct Metropolitan line from London in 1892. With the threat of closure already hanging in the air, ex-LNWR '1P' 2-4-2T No 46666 approaches Cheddington station with the 6.40 pm push-pull working from Aylesbury on 4 August 1949. The locomotive design dated from 1890, and several examples survived until the early 1950s without any rebuilding.

By January 1994 the former Aylesbury branch trackbed has been turned into the station approach road, while the Rosebery Arms still stands firm on the horizon. *H. C. Casserley/PDS*

AYLESBURY HIGH STREET: In 1950 the former LNWR Aylesbury terminus was renamed Aylesbury High Street in order to distinguish it from the main ex-GWR/GCR station in the town. Engaged in some light shunting at the terminus on 19 July 1952 is Ivatt '4MT' 2-6-0 No 43005.

The branch was closed to passenger traffic in February 1953 and to goods in December 1963. Today much of the route is difficult to trace as it has been incorporated into adjacent farmland, while the final station approach has recently been turned into a relief road. *H. C. Casserley/PDS*

LEIGHTON BUZZARD (1): Approaching Leighton Buzzard on the Up Fast line is 'Coronation' 4-6-2 No 46253 *City of St Albans* with the 'Merseyside Express' on 14 April 1962. No 46253 was one of 12 'Coronations' allocated at that time to Crewe North shed; the remaining 26 members of the Class were divided between other West Coast Main Line sheds at Camden, Carlisle Upperby, Edge Hill and Polmadie.

Locomotives at the south end of West Coast Main Line passenger trains became a rarity after the introduction of Driving Van Trailers in the late 1980s. Vehicle No 82121 heads a Wolverhampton-London Euston service through Leighton Buzzard on 31 December 1993. Although the main line here was resignalled in preparation for electrification in the mid-1960s, the LNWR signal box visible in the old photograph was retained to control shunting movements, and was not dismantled until 1976. *Stephen Summerson/PDS*

LEIGHTON BUZZARD (2): At the other end of the station, Stanier 'Black 5' 4-6-0 No 44829 races through producing its customary 'white feather' with a down relief train on 4 August 1962. On the left a Stanier '8F' 2-8-0 shunts the station goods yard. No 44829 was allocated at the time to Bushbury shed, while other members of this versatile Class were scattered throughout the London Midland Region as well as on former LMS territory in Yorkshire and Scotland. No 44829 was still in revenue-earning service in December 1967, but was not one of the dozen or so members of the Class to survive into preservation.

With the station platforms now lengthened and the goods yard site now occupied by commuters' cars, Class '90' No 90001 heads the 16.00 London Euston-Manchester Piccadilly express past the same location on 29 July 1992. *Stephen Summerson/PDS*

BLETCHLEY (1): Until the railway age Bletchley was a small village dominated by the adjacent market town of Fenny Stratford, on Watling Street. Bletchley's rapid expansion from the 1850s onwards was entirely because it lay on the new London & Birmingham Railway main line and was also the junction for Bedford, whereas the decline of Watling Street as a trade route led to the stagnation of Fenny Stratford. The original station buildings at Bletchley are pictured on 2 August 1956, complete with an Austin taxi and a Morris Royal Mail van.

The old buildings were swept away in the 1960s when the station was remodelled for electrification. The modern view is dated 9 August 1993. The importance of Bletchley as a junction declined with the withdrawal of passenger services to Oxford, Buckingham and Banbury, and its status as a calling point for West Coast Main Line InterCity trains was forfeited to the new Milton Keynes Central in May 1982. *Michael Covey-Crump/PDS*

BLETCHLEY (2): The view southwards from Bletchley station platforms was altered radically in the late 1950s by the building of Bletchley viaduct, designed to allow heavy freight traffic on the Cambridge-Oxford axis to keep clear of the West Coast Main Line. In the event, British Railways might as well not have bothered, because the expected growth in freight volumes never materialised. Restarting after a call at Bletchley on 7 August 1961 are English Electric Type 4 locomotives Nos D318 and D302 with the 6.40 am Wolverhampton-London Euston express.

Remodelling, resignalling and electrification have altered the view yet again. The power box on the right now controls 20 miles of the West Coast Main Line from Cheddington to Hanslope Junction. The ill-fated viaduct is now completely disused. Speeding through on the Up Fast line on 9 August 1993 is the 15.15 Birmingham New Street-London Euston service. *Michael Mensing/PDS*

BLETCHLEY (3): English Electric Type 4 No D330 passes through Bletchley with the up 'Royal Scot' in the summer of 1961. This locomotive type had a relatively short reign on the West Coast Main Line, taking over some previously steam-hauled services until the commissioning of electrification in 1966. No D330 was virtually new when pictured here; it later became BR Class '40' No 40130 and spent its last years working from Wigan Springs Branch depot until withdrawal in March 1982.

An up InterCity service passes the same location on 9 August 1993, headed by Driving Van Trailer No 82113. Trainspotting has almost become a thing of the past. *W. Turner/PDS*

BLETCHLEY MPD: In 1955 Bletchley shed still had an active allocation of some 45 locomotives, mostly involved in freight work and ranging from '3F' 0-6-0 tank engines to '8F' 2-8-0s. By the time of this photograph in 1964, however, the shed was very much in decline, as indicated by the line of mineral wagons parked in the building on the right. A solitary '8F' is in steam.

After the demise of steam the original shed was replaced by a new modern traction depot on the other side of the main line, with a sizeable allocation of electric and diesel multiple units and diesel shunters. The old shed site was used partly for car parking, while the tracks in the foreground continued in use as parcels sidings until the early 1990s. *G. L. Lane/PDS*

DENBIGH HALL has some historical significance as the temporary terminus of the West Coast Main Line from April to September 1838 while the section from here to Rugby was still under construction. In more modern times it marked the north end of Bletchley up yard, while the two tracks on the far right by-passed the yard to join up with the Bletchley flyover. An up mixed goods passes the junction on 16 August 1962, hauled by Stanier 4-6-0 No 45418 of Aston shed. This was one of the last locations between Rugby and London to remain uncluttered by electrification gantries.

The trackwork has remained intact, although the two right-hand tracks are by now well and truly covered by rust. Class '321' unit No 321416 forms an afternoon Milton Keynes Central-London Euston service on 24 December 1993. *Stephen Summerson/PDS*

BRADWELL: The 4-mile branch line from Wolverton to Newport Pagnell was opened by the LNWR in 1867, and Bradwell was one of the two intermediate stations. Right up to closure the line was steam-worked, passenger accommodation provided by a two-coach push-pull set of the same type as used between Leighton Buzzard and Dunstable (see page 92). Ivatt 2-6-2T No 41275 propels an afternoon working from Newport Pagnell at Bradwell on 14 June 1958.

The branch closed to passengers in 1964 and to goods in 1967. Today almost all of the trackbed has been turned into a footpath and cycle track, known as the 'railway walk'. Ironically the population along the line has increased dramatically with the development of Milton Keynes New Town, but there seems to be no prospect of the branch re-opening! *Stephen Summerson/PDS*

GREAT LINFORD was the other intermediate station between Wolverton and Newport Pagnell. A brief call is about to be made there by the 1.30 pm service from Newport Pagnell, propelled by Ivatt 2-6-2T No 41222, on 22 October 1963. There seems to be little custom; amazingly all three stations on the branch were still fully staffed at this time.

As at Bradwell, the platform edge at Great Linford is still there as a reminder of this leafy footpath's origins. Clearly a lot of money has been spent providing lighting, steps and a smooth tarmac surface. *Michael Mensing/PDS*

NEWPORT PAGNELL spent its 100-year life as a terminal station, although the original intention had been to extend the track eastwards to meet the Bedford-Northampton branch at Olney. Although that scheme was abandoned in the 1870s, some of the half-completed earthworks can still be seen to this day. Newport Pagnell itself had both passenger and goods facilities, and its passenger service in latter years comprised seven trains per day each way. Bletchley shed kept two Ivatt 2-6-2Ts for working the branch; No 41222 is seen here, after arrival with the 10.00 am service from Wolverton on 1 July 1963, as well as in the Great Linford photograph, while No 41275 was pictured at Bradwell.

Today the station site at Newport Pagnell is occupied by offices, as pictured on 17 June 1993. Both of the Bletchley 2-6-2Ts were eventually scrapped, although four other members of the Class survived into preservation. *David Holmes/PDS*

WOLVERTON: The LNWR main line of 1838 followed a more or less straight alignment through Wolverton. However, by the 1870s the line was flanked on both sides by the expanding LNWR railway workshops, and it was therefore decided to divert it to a new curving alignment some distance to the east; the new curve and station duly opened in 1881. This photograph shows a down semi-fast train via Northampton on 30 July 1963, hauled by Stanier 4-6-0 No 44744 of Longsight shed. Electrification works are evidently well advanced, although it was to be nearly three more years before a full electric service was introduced.

Class '321' unit No 321437 makes a call at Wolverton with the 16.50 London Euston-Northampton working on 9 August 1993. By this time the former station buildings on the road overbridge have been replaced by makeshift facilities off the left-hand side of the picture. Recently, with the running down of Wolverton Carriage Works, there has been talk of reverting the main line to its original alignment, but this would be a highly costly exercise and perhaps not justifiable in terms of the marginal increase in maximum train speeds. *Stephen Summerson/PDS*

Welwyn to Leighton Buzzard

WHEATHAMPSTEAD: The cross-country line from Welwyn Garden City to Luton and Dunstable was opened in 1860 and absorbed by the Great Northern Railway in the following year. In its early years it enjoyed through services to and from London King's Cross, but these were reduced because of competition from the shorter Midland Railway route between Luton and London St Pancras. In later years trains on the ex-GNR line had Hatfield as their starting and finishing point.

An interesting feature of the line in the late 1950s was the use of brand new diesel locomotives on local passenger trains, effectively a stop-gap measure until DMUs took over. Arriving at Wheathampstead on 26 September 1959 is Birmingham RC&W Co Type 2 No D5310 with the 3.48 service from Luton Bute Street to Hatfield. Soon

afterwards No D5310 was transferred to the Scottish Region which then became home territory for the entire Class. Under the TOPS renumbering scheme No D5310 became Class '26' No 26010, and it ended its career as a member of the ScotRail infrastructure fleet at Inverness in December 1992.

The former railway overbridge at Wheathampstead has disappeared in favour of a road widening scheme, but part of the station embankment is still visible on the left. *Michael Covey-Crump/PDS*

HARPENDEN EAST (1): Another locomotive type that spent most of its career in Scotland was the North British type 2, later known as Class '29'. However, the first 38 members of the Class spent their first two years working on former Great Northern and Great Eastern lines. During its short sojourn in the Home Counties, No D6104 arrives at Harpenden East station with the 2.30 pick-up goods from Hatfield to Luton on 26 September 1959. This train was scheduled to make a 28-minute stop at Harpenden East to shunt the goods yard.

Freight facilities were withdrawn from Harpenden East on 25 November 1963, while passenger services survived for another 17 months. Residential development now occupies the entire site. *Michael Covey-Crump/PDS*

HARPENDEN EAST (2): With Harpenden East goods yard now closed although still intact, a two-car Cravens DMU approaches the station with a morning Dunstable-Hatfield working on 16 May 1964. The passing loop is still controlled by GNR-pattern somersault signals.

Today a road runs almost exactly along the former trackbed, while 1970s housing occupies the land on the west side. *Michael Covey-Crump/PDS*

LUTON HOO: Passenger services were withdrawn from Luton Hoo at the same time as they were from the other stations between Welwyn and Dunstable, with effect from 26 April 1965. A two-car Cravens DMU draws to a halt at Luton Hoo with a morning Dunstable-Hatfield train on the last day of operation, Saturday 24 April 1965. After closure of this line, the Cravens DMUs remained a common sight on King's Cross suburban services until displaced by electrification in the mid-1970s. This particular batch of units then ended its days in East Anglia, with final withdrawals taking place in the mid-1980s.

Today the former station buildings at Luton Hoo survive in private ownership, and the trackbed at this point has been made into a public footpath.

The third picture shows an all too familiar sight on Britain's railways in the 1960s: the closure notice on display at Luton Hoo station in April 1964. *Michael Covey-Crump/PDS/Michael Covey-Crump*

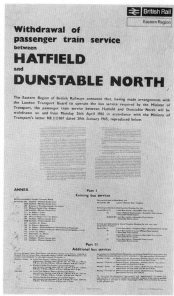

85

LUTON BUTE STREET (1): In British Railways days the ex-GNR station at Luton became known as Bute Street. To the south of Bute Street, the ex-GNR line ran alongside the ex-Midland main line, the signals of which can be seen on the far right of the photograph. A physical connection between the two lines had been authorised as long ago as 1863 but was not installed until over a century later in 1966. That was the year in which the line from Welwyn to Luton closed, but access needed to be maintained for freight trains between Luton and Dunstable. On 14 March 1959 GNR-design Class 'N2' 0-6-2T No 69577 sets off from Bute Street with a mixed goods for Hatfield. The old signal box was still in use at this time, but its replacement on the left is almost ready.

A visit on 6 August 1993 found little trace of the ex-GNR line through Bute Street, although amazingly a colour light signal was still lit beside the disused track just south of this point. *Stephen Summerson/PDS*

LUTON BUTE STREET (2): After the railways arrived, Luton's traditional hat-manufacturing industry gradually gave way to a wide range of engineering and chemicals industries, including Vauxhall Motors which opened its first factory in the town in 1905. Both ex-GNR and Midland lines were therefore well provided with rail-connected warehousing. Leaving Bute Street on 8 June 1962 is Ivatt 2-6-2T No 41289 with the 08.30 departure to Leighton Buzzard. This was one of the relatively few through workings over both ex-GNR (Luton-Dunstable) and ex-LNWR (Dunstable-Leighton Buzzard) portions of the route. They finally came to an end on 2 July 1962 when the line between Dunstable and Leighton Buzzard was closed. On the far right of the photograph are the remains of the GNR single-road engine shed, closed in the early years of the 20th century.

In 1994 it is hard to believe that a railway ever existed here. However, as recently as 1989 the line between Luton and Dunstable was still in regular use for freight traffic, and for a time in the 1980s it was earmarked in Network SouthEast's plans for re-opening to passengers and electrification. Such a re-opening now seems unlikely, given the estimated total cost of £12 million. *Stephen Summerson/PDS*

LUTON WEST: The railway from Welwyn to Dunstable was basically single-track, but there was a short double-track section from Luton Bute Street to Luton West. The driver of Class 'N2' 0-6-2T No 69547 is about to collect the single-line token for the section between Luton West and Dunstable on 29 September 1956. On the right are the sidings leading down to Henry Brown's timber yard, one of several railway goods terminals in the Luton area at this time. The GNR-design 'N2s' were a common sight on the Welwyn-Dunstable line until replaced by slightly newer 'N7s' from the late 1950s onwards. No 69547 was fitted with condensing apparatus and a small chimney, as it would originally have been used on suburban passenger trains over the 'Widened Lines' to Moorgate.

The Dunstable branch was re-aligned in 1988 to allow construction of the Luton-Dunstable relief road, pictured here on 6 August 1993. The 'new' track - by now disused - is almost out of sight, but runs between the concrete barrier and the high security fence on the left. *Stephen Summerson/PDS*

DUNSTABLE NORTH: The LNWR opened its branch from Leighton Buzzard to Dunstable in 1848. This line then became a through route after the GNR line from Welwyn was fully commissioned in 1860. Even in British Railways days, however, the two portions of the line were to a large extent worked separately. This scene at the former LNWR Dunstable station on 24 May 1962 shows Ivatt 2-6-2T No 41289 pulling out of the bay platform with a tea-time departure for Leighton Buzzard, while Class 'G2a' 0-8-0 No 49093 positions a van on the back of an afternoon departure for Hatfield.

A return visit on 27 July 1994 found the former station site occupied by council offices. *Stephen Summerson/PDS*

DUNSTABLE (M1 BRIDGE): Digging is well under way for one of Britain's first motorways in this picture dated 11 May 1958. Soon the remaining chalk embankment will be replaced by a bridge, to be built rather optimistically to double-track proportions. At the far end of the train is ex-LNWR 0-8-0 No 48953.

While traffic volumes on the motorway quickly exceeded all expectations, the railway entered a period of a gradual but irreversible decline. After the withdrawal of passenger services in 1965 and general freight services in the following year, the line was retained solely for bulk flows of cement and heating oil to Dunstable. The cement finished in 1988, although the Blue Circle sidings were not officially deleted from TOPS records until March 1991. Meanwhile the last delivery of oil from Thames Haven took place on 22 February 1989. The line was mothballed on 30 April 1989 and officially closed on 28 March 1991. *Stephen Summerson/PPS*

STANBRIDGEFORD was the only intermediate station on the 6¾-mile stretch between Dunstable and Leighton Buzzard. The usual two-coach push-pull set makes a call at Stanbridgeford on 28 April 1962 while forming the 5.30 pm Leighton Buzzard-Dunstable service, with Ivatt 2-6-2T No 41289 bringing up the rear. The distant signal is for the shunting frame that once controlled access to Totternhoe quarries.

Much of the trackbed between Stanbridgeford and Leighton Buzzard was swallowed up by the new A505 link road in the early 1990s. However, the new road gives a wide berth to the former Stanbridgeford station building which is now converted into a private house. *Stephen Summerson/PDS*

LEIGHTON BUZZARD (BRANCH PLATFORMS): Ex-LNER Class 'N7' 0-6-2T No 69644 prepares to depart from Leighton Buzzard with the 1.34 pm service to Luton Bute Street on 9 April 1958. The passenger accommodation comprises the rather unusual combination of a Gresley corridor Brake 3rd and a British Railways Mk1 vehicle. No 69644 was withdrawn later in 1958, and the 'N7' Class finally became extinct in 1961.

The location of the present-day scene can be verified by the chimney stacks in the centre of the picture. The new station building on the left was officially opened by the Marchioness of Tavistock on 20 May 1992. *David Holmes/PDS*

LEIGHTON BUZZARD YARD: The western end of the branch from Dunstable remained busy in its later years with bulk flows of sand and chalk. The latter originated at Totternhoe, between Stanbridgeford and Dunstable, and was conveyed in a daily block train to Southam cement works, near Rugby. Stanier '8F' 2-8-0 No 48360 is setting back into Leighton Buzzard yard with a healthy consignment of chalk on 30 July 1963. The flow came to an end in 1965 when replaced by a pipeline.

Sand continued to be conveyed by rail from the Dunstable branch until 1969, but after that there was little use for Leighton Buzzard goods yard and the site was eventually given over to car parking. Some of the cars' owners are no doubt on board the Class '321' unit, forming an evening rush-hour service from London Euston on 29 July 1993. *Stephen Summerson/PDS*

By Metropolitan to Aylesbury

HARROW-ON-THE-HILL: The original two-platform station at Harrow-on-the-Hill had been built in the 1870s when the Metropolitan Railway was bravely pushing its tentacles out into the green fields of Middlesex and Hertfordshire. With the rapid suburban expansion of the 1930s, traffic volumes increased substantially and the original double-track line was inadequate. Before long there was to be a total of six running lines between Finchley Road and Harrow-on-the-Hill, four for the Metropolitan Railway and two for the Great Central tracks out of Marylebone. The original Queen Anne-style station was a casualty of the expansion, being replaced by the modern structure, which is pictured here on 19 August 1951.

Changes to Harrow-on-the-Hill station in the intervening 43 years have been relatively few, but commercial development beside the station gives the scene a much more urban feel. A train of A60 stock makes a call while working a Watford-Baker Street service on 17 June 1994. *A. N. Davenport/PDS*

MOOR PARK: The Metropolitan Railway extended its tracks from Pinner to Rickmansworth in 1887. This section was electrified in 1925, and preparations were made for quadrupling the stretch between Harrow-on-the-Hill and Watford South Junction in the mid-1930s; in the event the quadrupling works were delayed by the outbreak of war. Arriving at the original two-platform Moor Park station on 10 September 1946 is a down Metropolitan train formed of 'T' Class multiple unit compartment stock. This stock was first introduced in 1927 and remained in everyday use until A60 vehicles took over in the early 1960s.

Quadrupling between Harrow-on-the-Hill and Watford South Junction was eventually completed in 1962, and Moor Park station was rebuilt with two island platforms. A train of A60 stock has just departed from the Up Slow platform while working a Watford-Aldgate service on 14 February 1994. *H. C. Casserley/PDS*

WATFORD: The 2¹/₂-mile branch to Watford was opened in 1925, and joined the main line at a triangular junction just south of Rickmansworth. Initially the branch was worked jointly by the Metropolitan Railway and the LNER by now the successor of the Great Central. But this duplication was soon considered to be wasteful and the Metropolitan took over completely within the first year of operation. Apart from the brief period of LNER steam operation, the Watford branch was worked by electric multiple unit stock from new. A 'T' Class train stands at the terminus on 16 October 1937.

The present-day photograph shows a basically unaltered Watford terminus on 28 July 1993. Looking at the map today, it seems as if the railway system between Watford and Rickmansworth is a classic example of bad planning. Within the space of 13 years new branch lines had been opened by the Metropolitan to Watford and by the LNWR to Croxley Green, yet although the lines passed within a few hundred yards of each other there was to be no physical connection nor any possibility of passenger interchange between the two lines. Today, with the Croxley Green branch now virtually closed in its present form, proposals first made 60 years ago to revive it and link the two branches have recently been resurrected, but this would obviously be a highly costly exercise and seems unlikely to go ahead unless the Government adopts a more enlightened attitude to public transport. *Tom Middlemass/PDS*

RICKMANSWORTH was the limit of electric operation for Metropolitan Railway trains from 1925 until 1962. During that period through trains were formed by hauled stock with electric traction between Baker Street and Rickmansworth and with steam traction between there and Aylesbury; the locomotive changes at Rickmansworth were claimed to be the fastest in the world! The two 'past' pictures show an afternoon Aylesbury-bound service undergoing its change-over on 8 April 1951. The incoming formation is headed by Metropolitan Railway 1,200 hp electric locomotive No 18. This was one of a fleet of 20 similar locomotives, reconstructed by Metropolitan-Vickers in 1922/23 from an original build introduced in 1904. The second photograph shows the ancient hauled compartment stock built between 1905 and 1923, which remained in use until the early 1960s, awaiting its steam locomotive.

Rickmansworth today is just an intermediate stopping point for Metropolitan line trains to Amersham and Chesham. A graffiti-ridden A60 formation is pictured with an Amersham-bound service on 28 July 1993. In addition to its Metropolitan line trains, Rickmansworth also enjoys a half-hourly BR service between Marylebone and Aylesbury.
A. N. Davenport (2)/PDS

CHORLEYWOOD: It seems hard to believe today that the Metropolitan Railway, later destined to become part of the London Transport underground network, once carried a substantial volume of freight. But by 1932 the Metropolitan was carrying annually some four million tonnes of merchandise and minerals and even operated goods depots at some of its outer suburban stations. The freight was steam-hauled, as illustrated by this photograph of Metropolitan 'K' Class 2-6-4 tank engine No 111 heading towards London on 2 June 1934. This was one of a Class of six assembled ten years earlier from parts made at Woolwich Arsenal for SE&CR-design 2-6-0s but incomplete when the war ended.

The Metropolitan relinquished its freight activities to the LNER in 1936. After the Second World War tonnages gradually declined, but some of the depots lasted a remarkably long time until final closures took place in 1966. Now the tracks through Chorleywood are well and truly passenger-only. Departing with a mid-morning Aylesbury-Marylebone service on 30 December 1993 is Class '165' unit No 165027. *H. C. Casserley/PDS*

CHALFONT & LATIMER: The Metropolitan Railway extended its tracks from Rickmansworth via Chalfont & Latimer to Chesham in 1889. The final section to Chesham then became a branch line when the main line was extended from Chalfont & Latimer to Aylesbury three years later. Arriving with the branch train from Chesham on 9 April 1960 is ex-LMS Ivatt 2-6-2T No 41329. By this time the live rails have already been installed on the main line towards Amersham, but they are not yet in use.

In 1994 Chalfont & Latimer retains its status as the junction station for Chesham, but locomotive-hauled trains have long since given way to London Transport A60 stock. The double-track junction illustrated in the earlier picture has given way to the customary single-track 'ladder'-type junction now preferred by signalling engineers. Platform-mounted mirrors are designed to permit one-person operation of London Underground trains; they also provide some opportunities for surreal photography! *Tom Middlemass/PDS*

CHESHAM (2): Before the arrival of the Ivatt 2-6-2Ts, the Chesham branch was worked by ex-LNER 'C13' Class 4-4-2T locomotives. Pictured running round its train at Chesham on 16 June 1951 is 4-4-2T No 67416, one of three members of the Class then allocated to Neasden shed. The ancient push-pull compartment stock, evidently not being used in push-pull mode on this occasion, went to the Bluebell Railway after withdrawal.

Goods facilities were withdrawn from Chesham in 1966, and the site of the goods yard and carriage sidings was later levelled to form a car park. The signal box was closed in 1970 when control of the branch passed to Chalfont, but it has clearly been well looked after since closure. The Chesham branch appears to have a relatively secure future, and it has even been suggested that Chesham might become a destination for trains using the yet-to-be-built Crossrail line. *A. N. Davenport/PDS*

AMERSHAM, or to give it its full title Amersham & Chesham Bois, is pictured on 22 June 1935 with Metropolitan Railway 4-4-4T No 107 hauling the 10.19 train from Great Missenden to Baker Street. At this time outer suburban trains such as this were steam-hauled north of Rickmansworth.

When the live rails to Amersham were energised in 1960, Metropolitan trains stopped running beyond this point, and the service to Aylesbury was provided entirely by British Railways trains running over Metropolitan tracks between Amersham and Harrow-on-the-Hill. In 1984 BR published its intention to close Marylebone and withdraw its service south of Amersham; if that proposal had been implemented Amersham would have ceased to act as a through station. Fortunately the intention to close Marylebone was reversed, and today the whole line is reaping the benefits of Network SouthEast's so-called 'total route modernisation'. Only on Sundays does the BR service stop short at Amersham, as pictured in this view of a Class '165' unit waiting to depart with the 14.34 service to Aylesbury on 13 February 1994. *H. C. Casserley/PDS*

AYLESBURY (I): The story of railway growth in the Aylesbury area is complex. Suffice to say that, apart from the 1839 LNWR branch to Aylesbury High Street (illustrated on page 68), all lines built to serve Aylesbury converged on a single station known in later years as Aylesbury Town. In 1907 this station became the jointly leased property of the Met&GC and GW&GC Joint Committees, reflecting its heterodox role. This general view of the station taken on 30 April 1961 shows the 10.05 am Nottingham Victoria-London Marylebone semi-fast calling at the Up Main platform while Fowler 2-6-4T No 42249 waits to depart with a London Transport train to Amersham.

Passenger services on the Chiltern Lines today are entirely in the hands of Class '165' 'Turbo' diesel multiple units, introduced in 1991. Unit No 165026 arrives at the much-rationalised Aylesbury station with a mid-morning train from Marylebone on 30 July 1993. *David Holmes/PDS*

AYLESBURY (2): Metropolitan Railway 4-4-4T No 107 departs with the 3.47 pm service to Verney Junction on 2 May 1936. This unlikely outreach of Metropolitan Railway operation came to an end just two months later, with the LNER taking over responsibility for all remaining passenger workings north of Aylesbury.

Fifty-eight years later the location is easily identifiable, and yet almost every detail of the scene has changed. The latest phase of modernisation was completed in the early 1990s and involved, amongst other things, the replacement of all remaining semaphore signals on the Aylesbury and Princes Risborough lines by colour lights controlled from Marylebone. The scheme also included major track alterations and the modernisation of all 23 stations on the two routes out of Marylebone. *H. C. Casserley/PDS*

AYLESBURY (3): The final pair of pictures at Aylesbury produces a contrast every bit as striking as the others, and yet the two views are separated only by 5¹/₂ years. In the first picture, Class '58' No 58034 propels the 09.15 Didcot-Aylesbury coal train along the extended siding leading to Aylesbury coal depot. The second track from the left is the freight-only line to Calvert, and on the right of the picture is the intact but disused public freight terminal. The sight of a Class '58' at Aylesbury was never commonplace, but occurred on several occasions during the period when Trainload Coal operated its own network for household coal traffic and sometimes used traction that was normally employed on 'merry-go-round' traffic. Aylesbury coal depot stopped receiving coal by rail in May 1989, although the sidings remained in use to handle limestone traffic from Mountsorrel until October 1990.

The setting for the second picture has changed almost beyond recognition in a remarkably short time. The site of the former goods yard is now occupied by a supermarket and car park, and the former area of wasteland on the west side of the line has become the new maintenance depot for the Chiltern Lines 'Turbo' fleet. Daytime freight through Aylesbury became scarce after the withdrawal of the Mountsorrel limestone trains, but in July 1993 the daily Avon household refuse train to Calvert and its return empties were rerouted via Aylesbury to allow mothballing of the lines between Calvert and Bicester London Road. Class '60' No 60041 approaches Aylesbury station with the 10.42 Calvert-Bath empties on 30 July 1993. This arrangement did not last long, as the mothballed route via Bicester was reopened in January 1994. *Both PDS*

North Buckinghamshire

QUAINTON ROAD (1): The first railway to reach the rural outpost of Quainton Road was the line between Aylesbury and Verney Junction, built by the Aylesbury & Buckingham Railway and opened to traffic in 1868. The second arrival at Quainton Road was the Wotton Tramway from Brill. It was not until 1899 that Quainton Road achieved real main-line status, with the opening of the Great Central Railway route from Nottinghamshire. The two branches from Quainton Road to Verney Junction and Brill were both closed before Nationalisation, leaving Quainton Road to eke out the rest of its existence as a quiet intermediate station on the Great Central main line. Approaching Quainton Road from the south is 4-6-0 No 73069 with a train of non-corridor suburban stock on 29 July 1961.

Quainton Road station was closed to passengers in 1963 and to goods in 1966, though the line between Aylesbury and Claydon remained open after that for through freight, parcels and empty stock movements. Today its only scheduled traffic is the nightly household refuse train from Northolt. Meanwhile Quainton Road station began a new existence in 1969 as the base of the preservation group then known as the Quainton Railway Society. Before long an impressive array of locomotives, carriages and other rolling-stock had been assembled for restoration and eventual display to the public, using siding accommodation on both sides of the BR line. The site is now known as the Buckinghamshire Railway Centre.
Stephen Summerson/PDS

QUAINTON ROAD (2): British Railways Standard 2-6-0 No 76036 passes Quainton Road with an up semi-fast train for London Marylebone on 29 July 1961. At this time ten examples of this mixed-traffic Class were allocated to Neasden for working on the Great Central main line.

North Buckinghamshire is a more sparsely populated area than the other areas depicted in this volume, so it is no mere coincidence that all of the 'present' pictures in this section illustrate railways that have either closed altogether or have remained open for very limited freight traffic. Nevertheless, at least the station at Quainton Road has been saved from the bulldozer and is now exquisitely maintained by the Buckinghamshire Railway Centre for the benefit of present and future generations. *Stephen Summerson/PDS*

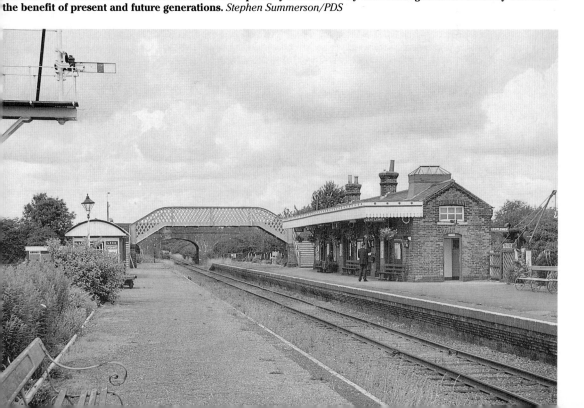

WADDESDON ROAD: One of the most curious railways to have ever existed in the British Isles was the Wotton Tramway, or the Brill branch as it was later called. It started out as a private tramway serving the estate of the Duke of Buckingham & Chandos, and the first section from Quainton Road station to Wotton opened for horse-drawn goods traffic only in 1871. Although the tramway was built to standard gauge there was originally no physical connection with the main line at Quainton Road. Within a year of its opening, the tramway was extended from Wotton to its eventual terminus at Brill, the horses were supplemented by steam locomotives, and some trains began to convey passenger carriages as well as goods wagons. Operation of the Wotton Tramway was passed on to the Oxford & Aylesbury Tramroad Company in 1894, but plans to extend it to Oxford never materialised. It was finally taken over by the Metropolitan Railway in 1899. Arriving at the intermediate halt of Waddesdon Road on 8 April 1933 is Metropolitan Railway 4-4-0 tank engine No 23, with the 1.00 pm service from Quainton Road to Brill.

Traffic on the Brill branch declined sharply in the early years of the 20th century. Speeds on the branch were low, and matters were not helped when the Great Western Railway opened an alternative station at Brill & Ludgershall on its main line between Princes Risborough and Aynho. The last train on the Brill branch duly ran on 30 November 1935. Today, however, much of the route can still be traced, despite the lack of heavy engineering works. At Waddesdon Road an unusually broad roadside verge marks the one-time course of the tramway. *H. C. Casserley/PDS*

112

BRILL: The makeshift terminus at Brill is pictured on 8 April 1933, with Metropolitan Railway 4-4-0T No 23 waiting to depart with the 3.07 service to Quainton Road. By this time passenger journeys on the branch were few, and the volume of goods had dwindled to around 20 tons a day. Traction on the branch in its final years was shared between two locomotives, Nos 23 and 41. Both were 'A' Class tank engines built by Beyer Peacock in the 1860s and had been used in their early years on the Inner Circle underground lines. No 23 was later renumbered L45 under London Transport ownership and survived after withdrawal in 1948 as a preserved locomotive, located first at the Clapham Railway Museum, then at the London Transport Museum.

There is absolutely no trace of the former tramway at Brill today. After closure the various assets of the line were quickly disposed of, and few people driving past the site today would ever dream that a standard-gauge railway track once existed here. *H. C. Casserley/PDS*

GRENDON UNDERWOOD JUNCTION: Heading towards London on the Great Central main line just south of Grendon Underwood Junction on 11 May 1964 is Stanier '8F' 2-8-0 No 48445 with a partially fitted mixed freight. Grendon Underwood was the point where the two alternative Great Central routes to London parted company, one running via Aylesbury and the Metropolitan line and the other running via Princes Risborough and the GW&GC Joint line.

Lineside undergrowth hides all but a brief glimpse of the remaining single track at the same location today. It sees only two regular train movements each day. Meanwhile the branch from Grendon Underwood Junction towards Ashendon remained open as far as Akeman Street for a weekly block train of fertiliser from Ince & Elton until May 1993; it is now officially closed. *Michael Mensing/PDS*

CALVERT: Located on the Great Central Railway main line between Quainton Road and Brackley, Calvert station was named after a local landowner, as there were no villages or towns nearby. Its typical GCR-style island platform had already been disused for a year when this photograph was taken on 11 May 1964. Ex-LNER 'V2' Class 2-6-2 No 60831 passes through with the 2.38 London Marylebone-Nottingham Victoria semi-fast train, while the down siding is occupied by a rake of highly distinctive Palbrick wagons, once used to carry palletised consignments of bricks from the adjacent works.

Rail-borne brick traffic from Calvert survived into the mid-1970s with a twice-weekly block train to Cardiff Canton as well as residual wagonload flows. The brickworks sidings then found a new use as a transhipment point for trainloads of containerised household waste, first from Northolt in north-west London and then from three forwarding terminals in the county of Avon. A rake of empty containers for Northolt can be seen awaiting collection in this photograph dated 30 July 1993. *Michael Mensing/PDS*

CLAYDON L&NE JUNCTION: In 1940 the pressure of wartime traffic led to the construction of a single-track connecting spur between the former LNWR and GCR lines at Claydon. This spur, in the right foreground of this 1970s photograph, allowed through working between Bletchley and Aylesbury without the need to reverse at Verney Junction. Movements on the spur were controlled by Claydon L&NE Junction signal box on the ex-LNWR line. Although the spur never supported a regular passenger service, it became a useful route for parcels and freight workings, plus occasional excursion trains such as shoppers' specials from Aylesbury to Milton Keynes, and movements of empty DMU stock between the Chiltern lines and Bletchley maintenance depot.

The ex-LNWR line from Bicester to Bletchley via Claydon was singled in 1985, but a loop was provided at Claydon so that trains could run between Aylesbury and Oxford without proceeding all the way to Bletchley to run round. The portable hut on the right is, believe it or not, the replacement Claydon L&NE Junction signal box, which was provided at the same time. The line between Claydon loop and Bletchley was mothballed in May 1993

after the loss of the last two freight flows using it; these were limestone from Whatley to Wolverton and fertiliser from Ince & Elton to Akeman Street. The line between Claydon and Bicester together with the wartime spur were also mothballed for the latter half of 1993, but these have since been brought back into use for the daily Avon refuse train. *Kevin Lane/PDS*

WINSLOW ROAD: Situated a good mile and a half away from the village of Winslow, Winslow Road was one of two intermediate stations between Quainton Road and Verney Junction on the line built originally by the Aylesbury & Buckingham Railway company in 1868; operations were taken over by the Metropolitan Railway in 1891. The 6.20 pm push-pull train from Aylesbury to Verney Junction is pictured calling at the typically deserted platform on 2 May 1936, with coach No 51905 being propelled by 2-4-2T 'Crystal Palace' locomotive No 8307. This locomotive was originally built for the Great Eastern Railway in 1909 as No 7596 and was renumbered 8307 in 1924. It was fitted with auto-gear and a vacuum ejector for working the Aylesbury-Verney Junction and Aylesbury-Princes Risborough lines, and continued to work on the latter route until 1940. It was finally withdrawn in 1943.

After the formation of London Transport in 1933, the Metropolitan Railway no longer saw the value of retaining a remote rural branch line in deepest Buckinghamshire. Winslow Road station was closed to both goods and passengers in July 1936, and the line between Quainton Road and Verney Junction was closed in 1947. By this time the alternative connection between the ex-Met&GC and ex-LNWR lines had been provided at Claydon. Today the site of Winslow Road station is occupied by the 'Station Kennels'. *H. C. Casserley/PDS*

VERNEY JUNCTION, like Calvert, was so remote from habitation that it took its name from the local landowner. But in railway operational terms it became an important interchange point between ex-LNWR and ex-Met&GC lines. The sign on the westbound platform tells the full story: 'VERNEY JUNCTION, JUNCTION FOR OXFORD & BANBURY BRANCHES AND METROPOLITAN LINES'. Ex-LNWR 'Cauliflower' No 8367 is seen arriving on 2 May 1936 with the 5.27 pm train from Bletchley to Banbury Merton Street.

Verney Junction was a rare example in the Beeching era of a station closing to goods before it closed to passengers. Goods facilities were withdrawn in 1964, while passenger services lasted until the closure of the Oxford-Cambridge line as a through route on 1 January 1968. The decaying station platforms are pictured on 28 March 1994, with the one remaining through track now mothballed. Happily not so decayed is the former station building, now in private ownership. *H C Casserley/PDS*

PADBURY: The LNWR opened its branch line from Bletchley to Buckingham and Banbury in 1850. In the early years of this century the line between Bletchley and Buckingham enjoyed a daily service of six down and seven up trains, with one train in each direction conveying a through carriage to or from London Euston. However, Buckingham failed to grow as a town, and by the mid-1950s its rail service was reduced to just three trains a day from Bletchley and four in the other direction. The line then became a test-bed for diesel multiple unit operation from 1956 onwards, using Derby lightweight single cars Nos M79900 and M79901. Car No M79901 ambles along just south of Padbury while working the 4.35 pm Buckingham-Bletchley service on 11 May 1964.

The same vantage point in July 1993 produces a very different result. The local farmer has made an excellent job of concealing the course of the railway! Only the outline of the hedge and the telegraph pole provide a link between the two views. *Michael Mensing/PDS*

BUCKINGHAM (1): No doubt the two Derby lightweight DMU cars would have caused quite a sensation at Buckingham when this photograph was taken on 27 October 1956. The British Railways Modernisation Plan had yet to take shape, and experiments with diesel traction up until this time had made only a very limited impact on the railway. But within ten years or so of this photograph almost every non-electrified local service in the country would be handed over to DMU operation, representing one of the biggest ever changes in British traction policy.

Unfortunately the introduction of experimental DMUs did little to improve the financial performance of the ex-LNWR branch to Buckingham and Banbury. The Buckingham-Banbury section closed to passengers in 1961 and to goods in 1963, while the Verney Junction-Buckingham section closed to passengers in 1964 and to goods in 1966. Part of the former trackbed through Buckingham has since been made into a public footpath. *Stanley Creer/PDS*

BUCKINGHAM (2): Ivatt 2-6-2T No 41222 of Bletchley shed shunts its two-coach push-pull set at Buckingham station before forming the 4.36 departure to Bletchley on 29 March 1958. The scene presents a delightful array of station furniture typical of the period, including portable wooden steps provided for passengers' use because of the low platforms.

No guarantees are given that this is exactly the same viewpoint in 1994! However, it illustrates the point that very little remains today of the former railway in Buckingham. *J. D. Edwards/PDS*

BANBURY MERTON STREET: The year 1850 marked the arrival of two railways in Banbury: the LNWR branch from Bletchley, and a broad-gauge line from Oxford promoted by the Birmingham & Oxford Railway. While the line from Oxford was destined to become an important through route, the LNWR line was only ever operated as a branch. The LNWR terminus was known in later years as Banbury Merton Street, and it is pictured on 27 April 1956 with British Railways Standard 2-6-4T No 80084 about to depart for Bletchley. On the right is a rake of cattle wagons, a common sight at Banbury because of the important cattle market in the town.

A return visit to the site of Merton Street station on 24 March 1994 found no trace of the former LNWR, but the location can be verified by looking at the roofline in the top right-hand corner of the picture.

The third picture shows the exterior of Merton Street station on 27 April 1956, still proudly advertising a railway company that had ceased to exist eight years previously. *Stephen Summerson/PDS/ Stephen Summerson*

Great Western lines

MARLOW: The first railway to reach High Wycombe and Princes Risborough was an initially broad-gauge line from Maidenhead in the Thames valley, opening as far as High Wycombe in 1854. Once High Wycombe gained its more direct link with London via Beaconsfield, however, the original line from Maidenhead became demoted to handling only local traffic. One of the intermediate stations was Marlow Road, later renamed Bourne End after becoming the junction for the Marlow branch in 1873. This 2³/₄-mile branch was opened with standard-gauge track, the 'main' line through Bourne End having been converted three years earlier. The Marlow terminus in its original form had one platform, four goods sidings and a goods shed. Great Western 0-4-2 Pannier tank No 1448 is in charge of the 'Marlow Donkey' on 21 June 1952.

The original station is commemorated today only by the 'Marlow Donkey' pub name, visible in the centre of the present-day photograph. The branch was cut back in 1967 to allow redevelopment of the site, and a new unstaffed platform was provided further down the line.

The third picture shows Metropolitan-Cammell two-car DMU Nos 51208 and 54402 arriving at the new platform with the 16.42 service from Maidenhead on 4 August 1993. This was one of the last first-generation DMUs to operate in the Thames valley and was itself withdrawn from service in the following month. *R. C. Riley/PDS (2)*

BOURNE END was still oozing with the atmosphere of a Great Western country branch line station when photographed on 13 July 1959 with the Marlow branch train arriving behind 0-4-2 Pannier tank No 1450.

The section between Bourne End and High Wycombe was closed to goods in 1967 and to passengers in 1970. Bourne End then became a reversing point on what was effectively a 7-mile branch line from Maidenhead to Marlow. Today's passenger service on the branch is, however, more complex than might seem possible at first sight. Off-peak, one unit shuttles to and fro between Maidenhead and Marlow, but at peak periods the unit shuttles only between Bourne End and Marlow, with through trains operating between London Paddington and Bourne End, using the second track and platform that have been retained at Bourne End. Pictured arriving with the 16.42 Maidenhead-Marlow service on 4 August 1993 is Metropolitan-Cammell two-car unit Nos 51208 and 54402. *Gavin Morrison/PDS*

GERRARDS CROSS: The 34 miles of railway between Northolt Junction and Ashendon Junction were built jointly by the Great Western and Great Central railway companies. The Great Western needed a shorter route between London and Birmingham compared with its existing line via Reading, while the Great Central needed an alternative approach to the capital to avoid using the busy and steeply graded Metropolitan line via Aylesbury. The first GCR expresses started using the new route between Northolt and Ashendon in 1906, followed four years later by those of the GWR. Storming through Gerrards Cross on 14 June 1958 is 'King' Class 4-6-0 No 6014 *King Henry VII* with the 6.30 am Birkenhead-London Paddington train.

From the 1960s onwards the joint line gradually lost its main-line status, becoming effectively a commuter line with all services operated by DMUs, and passing loops at intermediate stations were progressively removed. At Gerrards Cross the up line was slewed across on to the former Down Fast alignment, and a new up platform was provided in 1989. Class '165' 'Turbo' unit No 165034 calls with the 13.30 Birmingham Snow Hill-London Marylebone service on 15 February 1994. *H. C. Casserley/PDS*

BEACONSFIELD (I): Recalling the GW&GC Joint line's one-time role as a premier express route, 'Castle' Class 4-6-0 No 7013 *Bristol Castle* passes Beaconsfield with the down 'Cambrian Coast Express' on 20 September 1959. The 'Castles' were among the most successful locomotives of the Steam Age and remained in main-line service until displaced by diesel-hydraulics in the 1960s.

A humbler form of motive power provides the Joint line with its remaining passenger services today. Class '165' 'Turbo' unit No 165022 sets off from Beaconsfield with a lunchtime London Marylebone-Princes Risborough service on 28 July 1993. The through lines at Beaconsfield had been taken out of use as long ago as December 1973. *Gavin Morrison/PDS*

BEACONSFIELD (2): Although its construction was partly funded by the Great Central Railway, the Joint line between Northolt and Ashendon had an unmistakably Great Western flavour in terms of its station architecture and signalling. A typical GWR hipped-roof signal box and lower-quadrant semaphores greet 'Mogul' 2-6-0 No 5381 of Oxley shed as it passes through Beaconsfield with a London-bound mixed goods on 13 August 1956.

Freight services on the Joint line declined sharply in the 1960s and 1970s. The only scheduled freight trains through Beaconsfield in the summer of 1994 are a late evening trainload of household refuse from Northolt to Calvert and its associated return empties. A much simplified track layout sets the scene for this view of Class '165' 'Turbo' unit No 165022 bound for London Marylebone on 28 July 1993. *Gavin Morrison/PDS*

HIGH WYCOMBE (1): A feature of the Joint line in the early 1960s was the varied mixture of ex-GWR, ex-LNER and ex-LMS locomotive types in everyday use. Suburban services out of Marylebone were, until dieselisation, in the hands of ex-LMS 2-6-4 tank engines; No 42230 is pictured departing from High Wycombe with the 1.03 pm Princes Risborough-London Marylebone service on 30 April 1961.

The 2-6-4 tanks were made redundant by the arrival of four-car Derby diesel multiple units in 1962. They in turn were ousted by Class '165' 'Turbos' in 1992. 'Total route modernisation' has given High Wycombe a much simplified track layout, while the former down platform is now used by both down and up train services in order to provide better access for passengers. The down-side bay remains in use for terminating trains. Unit No 165021 departs from the bay with the 11.45 High Wycombe-London Marylebone service on 28 July 1993. *David Holmes/PDS*

HIGH WYCOMBE (2): Upon Nationalisation the entire Great Central system was allotted to the Eastern Region, and ex-LNER locomotives were therefore a common sight on services out of London Marylebone. It was only in 1958 that control of the former GCR main line passed to the London Midland Region. This photograph shows ex-LNER Class 'L1' 2-6-4T No 67747 approaching the up platform at High Wycombe on 4 April 1958, having just run round its train of suburban compartment stock.

The sharp curvature at High Wycombe was always a problem in steam days, necessitating a speed restriction of 35 mph on both up and down lines. Some improvement was possible when the tracks were realigned in 1989/90, with the result that speed restrictions are now 50 mph on the main running lines and 45 mph on the crossover. Entering High Wycombe station on 28 July 1993 is Class '165' unit No 165031 on a midday working from Banbury to London Marylebone. *R. C. Riley/PDS*

SAUNDERTON is a relatively minor intermediate station between High Wycombe and Princes Risborough. In steam days it had a service on the original ex-Wycombe Railway route from Maidenhead as well as trains from London Marylebone, and it was the Maidenhead service that retained steam haulage longest. Ex-GWR 2-6-2T No 6135 arrives at Saunderton with an afternoon Maidenhead-Aylesbury service on 8 June 1962; the new 4- and 8-car stop signs for DMU operation can be seen on the up platform.

Today Saunderton still has regular trains to and from Marylebone in the rush-hour, but at other times of day the service is sparse. Class '165' unit No 165037 passes through at speed with a morning working from Marylebone to Banbury on 4 August 1993. *Michael Covey-Crump/PDS*

PRINCES RISBOROUGH (1): In its heyday Princes Risborough marked the convergence of five railway routes, to London, Aylesbury, Banbury, Thame and Watlington. The branch to Aylesbury started out in 1863 as the 'main line' of the Wycombe Railway, but quickly became subordinated when both Princes Risborough and Aylesbury gained more direct links with London. Setting out from the Aylesbury bay platform at Princes Risborough is ex-GWR 0-6-0 Pannier tank No 6429 with the 12.55 pm push-pull working to Aylesbury.

Remarkably, all the lines radiating from Princes Risborough remained active until the late 1980s, and the Aylesbury branch has been fortunate enough to survive to the present day with a 2-hourly shuttle service from Princes Risborough and rush-hour trains to and from Marylebone. The curve of the Aylesbury line can just be seen in this photograph above the 15 mph speed restriction sign. *David Holmes/PDS*

PRINCES RISBOROUGH (2): With a Watlington branch train parked in the down bay platform, ex-GWR 'Hall' 4-6-0 No 5900 *Hinderton Hall* takes the Up Through line at Princes Risborough in charge of a Paddington-bound express on 23 July 1955. No 5900 was at that time allocated to Tyseley and would have been a common sight on Paddington-Birmingham expresses. After withdrawal in the mid-1960s No 5900 was rescued from the scrapline and preserved by the Great Western Society at Didcot. The photograph shows that the signals at Princes Risborough in 1955 were of the British Railways standard upper-quadrant type; in later years they were replaced by GWR-style lower quadrants. This is ironic considering that Princes Risborough was transferred from Western to London Midland Region control in 1974!

Today all passenger services at Princes Risborough are concentrated on the former up platform, with down trains using the crossovers at each end of the station; the former down lines are used only by engineers' trains. The magnif-

icent GWR-design signal box still stands, but all operational signalling is now controlled from Marylebone. The decline of the Joint line as a passenger express route was gradual but decisive: through trains to places such as Birkenhead were withdrawn in the mid-1960s; most London Paddington-Birmingham trains were rerouted via Oxford in 1973; and the very last scheduled locomotive-hauled working ran on 17 January 1992. A three-car Class '165' unit disappears into the distance with the 09.40 London Marylebone-Banbury working on 28 March 1994. *H. C. Casserley/PDS*

BLEDLOW BRIDGE: The 8³/₄-mile branch from Princes Risborough to Watlington was opened in 1872, and was a classic branch line serving a string of small rural communities. An afternoon working from Watlington is pictured approaching the tiny halt of Bledlow Bridge on 23 July 1955.

Passenger services were withdrawn from the Watlington branch in 1957. The section beyond Chinnor was closed completely in 1961, but the first 4 miles between Princes Risborough and Chinnor were retained until very recently as a freight-only line to bring trainloads of coal to the Rugby Cement works at Chinnor. However, the last railborne delivery of coal took place on 20 December 1989, and the line was officially mothballed by BR on 26 April 1991. *H. C. Casserley/PDS*

CHINNOR station is pictured on 23 September 1951, six years before the withdrawal of passenger services on the branch. In the foreground is the pointwork giving access to the Rugby Cement works, already a major user of the line by this time.

A return visit to Chinnor on 4 August 1993 found the pointwork for Rugby Cement still intact but no trace of the platform or station buildings. However, the line between Princes Risborough and Chinnor has been acquired for preservation by the Chinnor & Princes Risborough Railway Association, and permission to recreate Chinnor station on its original site has now been granted. Before long it is hoped to bring steam-hauled trains back to this delightfully picturesque line. *R. C. Riley/PDS*

INDEX OF LOCATIONS

BICESTER NORTH: 'Hall' Class 4-6-0 No 4907 *Broughton Hall* collects a slip coach detached from the 5.10 pm London Paddington-Wolverhampton Low Level express on the Down Through road at Bicester North on 31 May 1960. The station at this time still had two through roads and two platform roads, and a full complement of Great Western semaphores.

The 26-mile line from Princes Risborough to Aynho was the subject of an early rationalisation scheme in 1968. The track was singled except for a passing loop at Bicester North, and three intermediate signal boxes were closed. Then in 1992 the area came under the control of the new Marylebone signalling control centre. A peculiarity of present-day operations at Bicester is that both tracks have bi-directional signalling and it is therefore normal practice for trains to use the 'wrong' line. Unit No 165031 arrives on the former down line with an up train for London Marylebone on 30 July 1993, just as a down train waits at the former up platform! *Michael Mensing/PDS*

ASHENDON JUNCTION was the point where the Great Western and Great Central main lines parted company. The Great Central route to Grendon Underwood was built first, opening to traffic in 1905/06, and the Great Western line to Aynho and Banbury followed four years later. Because both routes were important, a flying junction was provided at Ashendon. On 27 August 1955 Class 'A3' 4-6-2 No 60102 *Sir Frederick Banbury* passes under the ex-GWR up line as it takes the ex-GCR route with the 12.15 pm express from London Marylebone to Manchester London Road.

The Great Central main line lost its prestige express trains in 1960, leaving just three daytime semi-fast workings in each direction, which were routed via Aylesbury instead of via Ashendon. The northern half of the Ashendon-Grendon Underwood link was retained for freight traffic to and from Akeman Street, while the southern half was used first as a diversionary route, then closed altogether. Once the ex-GCR tracks had gone from Ashendon, the remaining ex-GWR route was singled using the former down line, and the massive girder bridge that once carried London-bound Great Western expresses over the GCR route was removed. *Stanley Creer/PDS*

THAME (2): A modern 'past and present' comparison emphasises the sharp decline in BR's freight network in recent years. The BP oil distribution depot at Thame was considered until the 1980s to be a secure rail freight customer, with its daily deliveries of petroleum products conforming well to the BR ideal of high-volume full-trainload operation. But changes in BP's distribution patterns led to the untimely closure of this and several other terminals in the late 1980s and early 1990s. In happier times Class '47' No 47054 prepares to depart from Thame with the 7E54 empties to Shell Haven on 9 July 1986. Other sources of railborne oil to Thame in the 1970s and 1980s included the BP refineries at Grain and Stanlow.

Since closure in 1991 the Thame branch has quickly become weed-ridden, as this view of 28 March 1994 illustrates. *Both PDS*

THAME (1): Built by the Wycombe Railway to provide an alternative route between London and Oxford, the cross-country line between Princes Risborough and Oxford was opened to traffic in 1862-64. It was originally single-track and broad-gauge, but was relaid with standard-gauge track along with the rest of the Wycombe Railway in 1870. Despite offering a potentially shorter route between London and Oxford than the GWR main line via Reading, the line was not engineered to main-line standards and it never really prospered. Its passenger service was withdrawn in January 1963; with less than a year to go before closure, ex-GWR 2-6-2T No 6149 pauses with the 1.20 pm Oxford-Princes Risborough service on 25 August 1962.

Through freight traffic was eventually withdrawn from the Oxford-Princes Risborough line in 1967. A short section at the Oxford end remains in use to this day for automotive traffic to and from the Rover Group works, while the $5^3/_4$ miles from Princes Risborough to Thame was retained for bulk oil traffic until 1991. Today there appears to be no further use for the Princes Risborough-Thame section, and it can only be a matter of time before the track is torn up. *R. C. Riley/PDS*

WATLINGTON station was located amid green fields nearly a mile away from Watlington village. In view of the station's remoteness it is perhaps hardly surprising that the branch passenger service fell victim to bus competition in the 1950s. An unusually large gathering of passengers at Watlington station on 29 June 1957 indicates that this was the very last day of regular operation. Ex-GWR Pannier tank No 4650 is pictured shortly before departure with the 7.15 service to Princes Risborough.

Thirty-seven years later the platform is more or less visible through the undergrowth, and the station building still stands, but only just! *R. M. Casserley/PDS*